# SPIRITUAL ENCOUNTERS

## Testimonies from Healthcare Professionals

A LIFE Publication

IN ABUNDANCE THROUGH CHRIST

EDITORS:
**Elsa Vadakekut**
**Tony K George**

ASSOCIATE EDITOR:
**Rebecca Thomas**

INTERNATIONAL
EDITOR:
**Blessy Sucharita**

WESTBOW
PRESS®
A DIVISION OF THOMAS NELSON
& ZONDERVAN

WestBow Press books may be ordered through booksellers or by contacting:

WestBow Press
A Division of Thomas Nelson & Zondervan
1663 Liberty Drive
Bloomington, IN 47403
www.westbowpress.com
844-714-3454

Scripture quotations marked (NKJV) are taken from the New King James Version. Copyright © 1982 by Thomas Nelson, Inc. Used by permission. All rights reserved.

ISBN: 979-8-3850-2635-7 (sc)
ISBN: 979-8-3850-2636-4 (e)

Library of Congress Control Number: 2024910955

Print information available on the last page.

WestBow Press rev. date: 06/05/2024

# CONTENTS

# PREFACE

*Colossians 3:17 says, "And whatever you do in word or deed, do all in the name of the Lord Jesus, giving thanks to God the Father through Him." -New King James Version (NKJV)*

God has strategically placed us in various professions to represent Him. This book titled "Spiritual encounters in Healthcare" is a compilation of many testimonials of healthcare professionals who have experienced supernatural encounters while representing Christ at their workplace. Remember, Gideon had a supernatural encounter with the angel of God during his routine daily work of threshing wheat in the wine press. Similarly, our work becomes a calling when we are passionate about meeting the needs of the world around us. It is through this calling that God works in us and through us to convey His love to the people around us. People matter to God. Things of this world are not eternal, only people are eternal. Investing in the lives of people around us is critical as it defines their eternity, heaven or hell. Only a relationship with Christ will decide our eternity.

It is my prayer as we read these testimonials, God will enable us to be more sensitive to the needs of the people around us. And as we respond to those needs, we will have a chance to share God's love and point them to a relationship with Jesus Christ.

May the Lord use this book as an inspiration to many young or aspiring healthcare professionals to gain an eternal perspective, first and foremost, as ambassadors for Christ to a perishing world around them. I thank God for using each author towards contributing to this work and voicing their testimonies boldly for His glory. I thank the editors, Dr. Tony George and Dr. Elsa Vadakekut for their tireless and invaluable contribution in compiling and editing this book.

I hope and pray this book will be used for His glory and for the expansion of His kingdom.

Blessings,

**James Samuel, MD**
*President, Lukes' International Fellowship and Enrichment (LIFE)*
*Pastor, Redeemer's Church of Connecticut, Bridgeport, CT*

# FOREWORD

I consider it an honor and privilege to write a foreword on this valuable book, *"Spiritual Encounters: Testimonies from Medical Professionals"* highlighting the spiritual insights of young doctors in their quest to serve their patients patterned according to the teachings of the Great Physician, our Lord Jesus Christ. The prime requisite of anyone willing to follow Lord Jesus, the Leader Par Excellence the world has ever seen, is stated in Lord Jesus' own words:

> *"If anyone desires to come after Me, let him deny himself, and take up his cross, and follow Me"*
> *(Matthew 16:24, NKJV)*

Young people pursue a medical career for many reasons. Being successful in a medical career involves great sacrifice, hours of hard work and extensive study. Very few professionals have the aim of serving the people as their prime motive, but in a competitive world where 'success' is a catchy word, and many people are in the rat race for reaching a top position, humanitarian service takes a back seat.

Across the pages of this book, you will find the life stories of medical professionals who have taken the challenge of ignoring the worldly pursuit of achieving fame and pursuing their vocation with one aim of offering their talents to the welfare of the patients who seek their help at a great cost of abandoning a comfortable life which they could have otherwise enjoyed. But the real question is why and how these intellectuals could sacrifice their lives, especially when surrounded by criticism from their colleagues and even their own kith and kin, who may not understand their motives. As you read these stories of young doctors looking at their profession as a means to serve others, there is one common compelling factor that led them into this "dare to be different". That single motivating stimulus is our Lord Jesus Christ.

A passionate understanding and appreciation of the mission of Jesus is probably the most important motivating factor that helped men and women of all ages in the last two thousand years of human history to involve in humanitarian services in manifold ways and has made this world a better place to live in especially for the destitute, the poor, the hopelessly sick and the needy people.

Loving Jesus means loving those around you who are in need of help. Jesus said "Assuredly, I say to you, inasmuch as you did *it* to one of the least of these (the poor, the naked, the hungry, the thirsty, the bonded, the slaves etc...) My brethren, you did *it* to Me (Mathew 25: 40, *NKJ Version*). Accepting Jesus' sacrifice as a ransom for our sins and for our redemption and salvation will lead us to involve in selfless sacrifice for others. That is the mystery behind the life of every story you will read in these pages.

A small reminiscence of my own life's transformation will vouch what I am saying. Way back in 1966, when I was a medical student, I had an encounter with the Lord Jesus in a mysterious way and ever since that experience, He became my role model. One aspect of Jesus' life that really attracted me to Him was His concern for the poor. This is because the day I met Him I was in the midst of some poor people in a small prayer meeting. I was overwhelmed with the thought that the Creator of heaven and earth and the Almighty God could be there in the midst of that small group of poor people. Then, the more I studied the life of Jesus, the more I was convinced that Lord Jesus, during his earthly ministry, was more biased towards the poor. Even though every aspect of Jesus' character is worth emulating, this character trait of His was the one that gripped my life and became a bottom-line truth for following Him. I decided if Jesus' heart was with the poor, I would have His constant companionship if I also worked with the poor. And for the last 40 years, my family and I moved to work among the most neglected tribal groups. Looking back at these 40 long years of living with a poor tribal community, I can honestly say that my conviction that my Lord Jesus was with me was the most assuring reason that I could enjoy working with them. The whole 40 years of ministry along with God, was evidenced by the miraculous provisions of God meeting every need in the mission field. I would not venture to trade this experience with any other form of service because all along I have been witnessing the miracle working Hand of God.

I hope the wonderful compilation of the experiences of forty young Christian medical professionals that fill the pages of this book will inspire many readers to dedicate their lives to help needy patients and their relatives and to point them to the Great Physician of all times, our Lord Jesus Christ.

God bless all the readers,

**Dr K. Muralidar, MD**
*President, Inter Collegiate Prayer Fellowship*
*President, Bethany Medical Center*

# JESUS IN THE MOMENT

## Toby Abraham, DO

I can detail the overwhelming feelings of being a fresh new attending in a new hospital. One of my first patients was an elderly, cachectic patient with bladder cancer. He was known to that floor as a man of few words and with a flat affect. He was severely underweight and malnourished, weighing less than ninety-five pounds. The surgical and oncology consultants deemed his prognosis grim and non-curative. There was nothing else to do. Finding a living arrangement for him became a complicated issue, and that is when we met. I saw him several days in a row. Initially, he wouldn't look me in the eye and he would respond with a flat yes or no or "I feel fine."

My father passed away from metastatic cancer less than 2 years ago. Oddly enough, although different ethnicities, he had resemblances that reminded me of my father. I knew this man would die in days to weeks, and I couldn't do anything about it—this alone was humbling. The Lord started working in my heart to be intentional with him. As days went on, I spent a few extra minutes with him. He began to say things that surprised me, such as

"I used to believe in Jesus" and "I find it odd to pray." He also told me no one ever liked him enough to marry him. Eventually, he admitted, "I'm not used to compassion; I'm lonely."

I started talking to him about his faith and Jesus. But he was almost dismissive. He would listen but was hesitant and resistant. On my last day working, I finally prayed with him. After praying, I realized I may never see him again. He lay there with a blank face. I nearly walked out, but the Lord encouraged me to stay and engage with him more. And then, in that moment, my heart filled with compassion. As I spoke and looked him in the eyes, tears falling freely down my face, I told him there was nothing else we could do medically for him and that his life would likely end shortly. And in that moment, the Lord allowed me to share the pure and eternal Gospel and the weight of its meaning personally for him, despite the hopelessness of his situation. For the first time, he looked me eye to eye and said, "Thank you! Thank you!"

I don't know about his outcome, and I've never seen him since. But we encountered Jesus in that moment. The Lord led, I followed. And even if his life was about to end, the peace of sharing the eternal truth in a seemingly hopeless situation when all else was lost, was palpable at that moment, and it was an experience I'll never forget.

# COMPASSION

## Sharon Cynthia, MD

In the labor ward that particular night, the putrid smell was overpowering, hitting me with a wave of nausea as soon as I entered the room. It smelled like death. I asked the nurses what it was and they pointed to an almost lifeless form on the triage bed - the reason they had called me in the middle of the night. I rushed over and found a young girl with cold, clammy skin and a thready pulse, gasping for air. The woman next to her would not open her mouth when I asked her what happened. After starting emergency treatment, I called for help. The young girl was taken to the operation theatre where several liters of pus were removed from her abdomen and she had several units of blood transfused. The operating surgeon found four holes punched in her uterus which were repaired. The girl did not wake up after the surgery and was on a ventilator for nearly a month.

Except for her elderly mother, the rest of her family never came after the first day. We kept asking the mother what happened and she finally narrated the story. This was 14-year-old Daya (name changed) who had been abused by her brother-in-law and had conceived a child. The family took her to a fraudulent doctor who attempted an unsterile method of abortion and punched four holes in Daya's uterus. After a few days, when her abdomen was filled with pus, she was brought to our hospital. Whenever the weekly bill was handed to her mother, they would ask if we would disconnect the ventilator so they could take her home. Every time I would see Daya's almost lifeless body in the ICU, I would ask God why He had let this happen.

In spite of the brutal back story, the time that Daya spent in the ICU was one of my several first-hand experiences to understand the meaning of the word compassion. The team of doctors never gave up on her. They gave her the best care possible in the limited circumstances irrespective of the cost. The nurses wept and prayed over Daya's nearly lifeless body daily as they cleaned her excreta and sponged her frail body. The dietician came up with the best possible tube feeds. The administrators knew that the whole cost of her treatment, nearly 1.5 lakhs, would be borne by the hospital. I remember the morning review meetings when the director prayed and made a decision to continue her treatment. This child whom no one cared for was loved in the most basic yet powerful way possible. After a few days with Daya, my posting was changed to another department and I would only hear occasional updates about her.

Nearly a month had passed and I can never forget the day when I was sitting in OPD (Outpatient Department) in the middle of a sea of patients and I saw a smiling face. I could not recognize the patient. My heart skipped a beat and I jumped out of my seat when I realized it was Daya. She had recovered completely. What surprised me more than her survival was that she had joy and hope in her eyes. In the most painful period of her life, Daya had received Jesus and she received life, in its most abundant sense.

Through Daya's survival, I saw, heard and witnessed compassion. *Compassion* means "to suffer together with". It is a feeling that motivates one to go out of his/her way to relieve the physical, mental, or emotional pain of others and themselves. The difference between sympathy and compassion is that the former responds to others' suffering with sorrow and concern whereas the latter responds with warmth and care.

In the Old Testament, we come across compassion as the fundamental character that God identifies as His. Exodus 34:6, *NKJV* - "And the LORD passed before him and proclaimed, the LORD, the LORD God, merciful and gracious, long suffering, and abounding in goodness and truth, keeping mercy for thousands, forgiving iniquity and transgression and sin." This revelation was at a time when the nation of Israel had made a golden calf just 40 days after their miraculous escape from Egypt and Pharaoh. We see God as a trailblazer in compassion towards orphans, widows and sojourners. What unites the widow, the orphan, and the sojourner as a special focus of God's merciful attention? The answer to this question is vulnerability. These people groups shared political, social, and economic vulnerability in a society which did not consider them as humans. They were frequently poor and commonly oppressed, abused, and disadvantaged.

In today's world, these are unborn babies, migrant workers, pregnant girls out of wedlock, and the sick and suffering in our church. In the Old Testament, God advocated for their care when other people or systems of social protection failed. In the New Testament, through the person and work of Jesus Christ, we see the compassion of God incarnate. Jesus touches the untouchable leper. He weeps at the deaths of the widow's son in Nain and his close friend Lazarus. Jesus is filled with compassion on seeing the multitude as they were like sheep without a shepherd. As God reveals more of His fullness, we see the character of the good shepherd reaching out to the one wayward sheep. Today, who is the leper whom we are afraid to go near? Who is that wayward sheep, God is asking you to go after?

In the epistles, in Colossians 3, the new man is asked to put on the clothing of compassion. When you were getting ready to come to church this morning, you had to put off the night clothes and put on the church clothes. Similarly, Paul asks the believers at Colosse to put off many unwanted attributes anger, slander, sexual immorality and covetousness and put on compassion, kindness, humility, meekness and patience. Compassion is "...a multidimensional process comprised of four key components: (1) an awareness of suffering, 2) sympathetic concern related to being emotionally moved by suffering, (3) a wish to see the relief of that suffering, and (4) a responsiveness or readiness to help relieve that suffering". So, do you want to put on compassion?

Once our spirit is made alive in Jesus, we have the privilege of putting on compassion every day. Though we are made alive in Christ by faith, putting on compassion is a daily choice – just like the choice of clothing we made today. How can I make that choice? As it says in Galatians 2:20, *NKJV-* "I have been crucified with Christ; it is no longer I who live, but Christ lives in me; and the *life* which I now live in the flesh I live by faith in the Son of God, who loved me and gave Himself for me."

Putting off the old man requires being crucified with Christ. Carrying the cross with Jesus may sound like an abstract idea. For me, the cross may be the clutter of files on my office table and the pile of dirty dishes waiting in my kitchen while I am taking a few extra minutes to hold a patient's hand as she cries. Consciously prioritizing time, effort, money and prayer for another person who can never repay me back requires putting my priorities on the cross.

Thankfully, Jesus has already carried His cross and mine. Hence, in an unexplainable contradiction, as I step forward to be crucified with Christ, I am actually invited to a state of restful obedience with a light yoke and an easy burden. Further, when I received Jesus into my heart, I am sealed with the Holy Spirit who empowers me with the same power that raised Jesus from the dead. He empowers me to make the choice of putting on compassion every morning as I read His Living Word and kneel before Him in adoration, even before I get out of bed.

# DISCOVER YOUR DESIGN

## Stephen Digal

Parents and children share one of the strongest bonds in human history. Sometimes scrutinized and sometimes enclosed with controversies, it is obvious that not all parents share the perfect bond with their children. It is uncommon for parents to reject their child. Sometimes parents reject their child because of their failed marriage. My parents separated when I was a toddler. This disturbing reality had a brutal impact on me and my relationship with my parents. For me, dealing with rejection was tough and emotionally challenging and feeling unloved and unwanted was a regular experience. I was shocked when my father married again. Even worse, my step mother never loved me. I recall the physical and verbal abuse I went through then. The trauma and agony were unbearable. Instead of love, I was abused, instead of care I was kicked, instead of loving arms I was beaten with brooms. Parental involvement is fundamental to a child's growth but it wasn't for me. Even though my father was aware of these happenings, he turned a blind eye.

I lived with my family for 3 years, when my aunt

observed the abuse and took it in prayer. She decided to move me to a children's home run by American, British and Filipino missionaries. I got a new name and a new identity. I was delighted! I had the best food, clothes, care and friends to play with. Us orphans were now brought up in conservative Christian homes. We had guidelines to love and give love and consequences if we disobeyed. We were taught to love and care for each other. Now I was growing up having good friends, spiritual surroundings and people I adored. We all had sponsors who made sure our needs were met. My attention was fixated on the missionaries and their lives, and I started enquiring 'Why am I here?' I started to realize these missionaries didn't have biological children but they loved us as their own. What made them do that? Who is creating this behavior? These were questions propelling me to dive deep to understand them.

The morning devotions guided us through the day, while the chores and activities taught us to live practically in this world. The evenings were a time of evaluation, where I realized I was not alone and had someone to care for me. After dinner, there was a feeling of security and care, feeling loved and being felt precious. My best lessons in life came during my stay at the children's home with the missionaries. I forgot 'the past' and focused on 'what is to come'. At a tender age I received my calling and reminded myself 'I was special'. I needed inner healing and coming out of that pain was difficult and demanding. Gradually I found my past hatred and hurt vanishing. The missionaries and their commitment compelled me to draw nearer to the needs of the people, to be the voice to the weary, poor and needy.

The time spent in the Children's home is transfixed in my heart, never to be erased. It taught me to love and to care, to stand strong and to discover my design. The mission trip to the Philippines opened my eyes. Since then, I have travelled throughout India standing with the poor and destitute any way I can. I know where I come from. I know how missions and missionaries have transformed the way I looked at rejection. I know who laid a strong foundation for them. Their prayerful knees and helping hands and Christ's love magnified affirmed my design.

# HOLY SPIRIT, LEAD!

## Joel Finny, MD

*"Blessed be the LORD my Rock, Who trains my hands for war, And my fingers for battle"*
*Psalms 144:1, NKJV*

I pray that whoever reads this spiritual encounter is transformed by the Spirit of God to skillfully engage the enemy, binding up the strong man and plundering his goods for the Father's glory. My first encounter with Mr. DW started poorly as I was about 20 minutes late to the phone appointment. He began the conversation full of expletives on how the VA is not appropriately compensating him for all the suffering he went through in military service and the effects of trauma on his mental health continuing to disable him. His question to me was, what would I do about it? After several unsuccessful attempts to speak and explain that this was not my role, he would enter into a barrage of expletives followed by a list of medical problems covering probably 20 chief complaints without giving me any chance to ask clarifying questions. The follow-up calls with Mr. DW were typical of the first appointment, each full of anger and verbal lashings.

After several such occasions, I dreaded seeing his name on the schedule. Besides, I began questioning my heavenly Father why He would allow me to endure such situations. Didn't He care? I believed many prophetic promises, but my eyes could not see how this encounter was leading me to fulfill any of them. In many ways, I was crying the same cry the Israelites cried in the wilderness when there was no sign of a promised land.

Couldn't He simply remove this person from my care? On one occasion, I tried to get him reassigned to another team, but it was unsuccessful. Like Jonah trying to run the other way, my best attempts were useless against an Almighty God. One day, as I was sitting in my office, thoughts of bitterness through this wilderness experience began consuming my mind when the Helper reminded me that I had asked for treasures in darkness but belonging to my Father, treasures hidden to the eyes of men but not to the eyes of my Heavenly Father. Indeed, I did ask Father to work among those who are oppressed mentally, those who battled addiction to drugs, alcohol, and whatever the enemy has used other tools to enslave in his kingdom. He also delivered the scripture to me from Jeremiah 12:5, NKJV- "If you have run with the footmen, and they have wearied you, Then how can you contend with horses? And *if* in the land of peace, *In which* you trusted, *they wearied you,* Then how will you do in the floodplain of the Jordan?" This was a challenge resembling the words of Jesus to the large crowd following Him, to whom he reminded to count the cost and gave a parable of a person building a tower and a king calculating the difficulty of warring against someone two times the size of his army. The Helper who delivered this word opened through it a way of escape from the " why me, don't you care " thoughts attempting to choke out the promise. What a Helper, the Holy Spirit!

Then, one day, the front staff sent me a message Mr. DW was here in person and wished to speak with me about an issue. Without hesitation, I said yes as the word equipped me with confidence in my Father and His purpose for me. My imagination created a large, monstrous, imposing figure; however, much to my surprise, my vain imagination was false, and he was a shorter man, wiry thin, and did not look as he sounded on the phone. During the conversation, he shared about the scripture, and not long after, the Holy Spirit opened a door into this man's heart just as Lydia's heart opened to the gospel's message. It was my Father speaking to Him and placing the right words in my mouth, bringing life that comes by the Spirit directly into his heart. The Holy Spirit reminded him of the fullness of joy, peace that overflows, and love that never ends found in a relationship with the Heavenly Father fully restored when Jesus Christ declared, "It is finished." No more separation exists for anyone who puts faith in the person of Jesus Christ as he is immediately adopted into sonship and given the gift of the Holy Spirit to remain with him until Christ returns. His eyes brightened and it was clear that he was not expecting to hear such words. The Spirit gives life, and this new covenant ministry is a work of our Heavenly Father and marvelous in the eyes of men. Our Father doesn't just forgive us as the scriptures teach us, but those who repented and were baptized not only received forgiveness and salvation by grace through faith but also His gift!

Our relationship changed from that moment, and he apologized profusely, asking for forgiveness for his past behavior towards me. I reassured him he was forgiven just as I had been forgiven, and the One who forgives fills us with a love that can forgive any offense. We prayed together, I purchased lunch for him that day, and we ate together. Recently, I was reading about the exploits of David's mighty men. They were men who exhibited extraordinary bravery and accomplished incredible feats beyond human imagination or ability. However, reading about the beginnings of these men is even more surprising. Before encountering David, they were considered outlaws, societal misfits, complainers, and those with no semblance of a righteous mold. However, through the influence of a man after the Father's own heart, these men became battle-tested renowned warriors through training in battles. Is this not what Jesus did with those who followed Him? Did He not take a bunch of no-knowns into men who turned the world upside down? Did he not take society's outcasts, such as Mary Magdalene and the demoniac from the region of the Gadarenes, and grant them freedom and grace to proclaim the truth that set them free? Is this not the same mission for which we have been commissioned by our Heavenly Father and fully equipped by the Holy Spirit? Yes, there will be weary days where you want to put the plow down, but the Spirit will intercede as those who the Spirit trains will find new, hidden strength to continue plowing and not look back! Be strengthened by the Spirit of God to continue plowing for His Kingdom, by His power, for His Glory!

# A TEACHER WHO CHANGED MY LIFE

## Phillip Finny, MD

Teachers are someone we look up to and often revere. Along my life's journey I have had the privilege to be instructed and taught by many wonderful teachers and I am what I am today due to many of their sacrificial inputs in my life.

Although there are many names that come to my mind of some of my best teachers at school and at college, there is one individual who has been perhaps the most instrumental in inspiring me to be who I am today. He was and continues to be my mentor and role model over the past 30 years. Let me share some of the reasons why he played such a pivotal role in my life.

It was August 1990, and it was the sponsorship body meeting at the Scudder Auditorium premises of Christian Medical College- Vellore (CMC). Dr. Colin Binks, FRCS, represented my sponsoring body and he interacted with us medical students from our sponsoring body. He was a gentle British surgeon working in a tribal region of Jharkhand for over 10 years. He spoke passionately about the exciting ministry they were involved in. He concluded by extending an invitation to all of us to consider visiting the mission hospital where he was serving for a short period during our vacation. This thought stayed in my mind and was reinforced when we received a Christmas card and a personal letter in December 1990. My friend and I decided to spend two weeks of our summer vacation with Dr. Binks and his team in the Palamau district of Jharkhand. This is one of the poorest regions in India and a Naxalite dominated area. We went and spent two memorable weeks with him and his team. I was inspired by the wonderful work done by the medical team among these poor tribals and seeing firsthand the servant leadership of this doctor. Even though I was only a first-year medical student, I was encouraged to take deliveries under supervision and assist in major and minor surgeries which both thrilled and motivated me to study better as I realized the necessity to study anatomy and other basic sciences well.

After this visit, my academic performance at CMC significantly improved and I no longer studied for my grades or marks, but with the awareness that if I do not study well, I could potentially endanger the life of my patient. I topped my class in the second MBBS and the mission hospital visit at the end of the first-year exams was perhaps the most significant turning point for me. Through the rest of my course at CMC, Colin continued to write personal letters every year around Christmas time and occasionally call me on phone to enquire of my well-being. I found this most surprising that such a senior surgeon, who was literally revered in that part of Bihar, should be so genuinely concerned about me and keep in constant touch.

After my MBBS course, to my pleasant surprise I was posted for my bond to this same hospital. I now had the opportunity to be directly working with Dr. Binks and to sharpen my clinical skills and in particular, to gain surgical experience. He patiently taught and assisted me on various surgeries including c-sections, laparotomies and other gynecological procedures. His calmness and encouraging words built me up and I soon became a confident young "surgeon" within a year. At the end of my first year, I heard the news that I was being transferred to another hospital in our mission network. I was indeed upset, but Dr. Binks was a great comfort. He and his wife took me home for a meal with hot coffee and prayed with me. They promised to quickly prepare me before I went on my next assignment to assist a CMC trained physician who was struggling alone in another busy mission hospital in Assam. I was given every opportunity to operate in the ensuing 2 months before I left the hospital to improve my confidence. On the penultimate day before I left, Dr. Binks realized that I had not managed a patient with intestinal obstruction and lacked the ability, skills to do a resection and anastomosis which can be life-saving for a patient with intestinal obstruction. The next day morning, hours before I left, Colin arranged for one of his pet rabbits to be sacrificed and the bowels arranged in the backyard to be used by me to practice resection anastomosis along with him as my teacher. This unique experience moved me to tears. This level of commitment to go the extra mile to train a young doctor to completely equip him was unbelievable. In the second hospital where I served, all the practical training that I received under Dr. Binks helped me immensely.

I realized that God had called me to be a physician through these rich experiences during my sponsorship obligation. Colin encouraged me to apply for General Medicine and over the past 24 years has continued to remain in touch with me regularly. Every Christmas season I get a handwritten letter and a card from him. We talk on phone even now, occasionally.

Why do I consider Dr. Binks as the teacher who changed my life? He epitomized the description of a servant leader for me and he remains my role model. He poured out himself completely to train me and went the extra mile to do things which no ordinary teacher would take the time or effort. His humility and gentleness made a huge impact on me. Even though I was only a fresh medical graduate, he would come and discuss cases to seek my opinion. This was most unusual, and I found him to be willing to learn from a novice like me. His actions spoke louder than words. The soothing words he spoke to our anxious and agitated patients in Bihar taught me how to handle an angry and difficult patient. He gave the credit often to his junior doctors and preferred to support them from behind. This revealed his commitment to build up and train others. He has walked alongside me all these 30 years from the time I joined medical school. He is now retired and went back to the UK several years ago but continues to be interested in my personal and professional progress. I have seen firsthand the legacy he left in tribal Jharkhand when he retired.

In my life choices, I was inspired to follow his footsteps my giving the first ten years of my career after my postgraduate training to serve in mission hospitals in Bihar and Assam. In this period, I also tried to pass on the baton I received from Dr. Binks to build up the next generation of doctors who are willing to serve in these remote parts of India. My life journey was most influenced by my meeting this gentleman and I feel so fulfilled today as I look back at life. He never tried to control me in my career choices but always sent me with his blessings especially when I had to return to CMC for my postgraduate training. Dr. Binks was truly a signpost in my life.

As I work today and enjoy my role as busy clinician and a teacher, I am reminded of the need to sacrificially train my younger colleagues and to be available to them. The importance of continuing to journey with them even after we part ways is a lesson I learned from Dr. Binks. They say "**values are caught and not taught**". I imbibed many such values by observing him in action. One of the priceless lessons I learned was the tremendous dependence on God Dr. Binks had during surgeries. He would always start the surgery with prayer, asking for God's strength to perform the surgery even if was the most common surgery like a c-section.

In conclusion, I feel my best teacher walked his talk and selflessly gave of himself to equip me when I worked with him and even after we parted ways. The well-known quote "**we are standing on the shoulders of giants, that is why we are able to see further**" is apt to quote in this context. Truly, he allowed me to stand on his shoulders and encouraged me to take the road less travelled. My life and career trajectory were greatly influenced by meeting Dr. Binks. Today I am convinced that his example has changed me and made all the difference in my life.

# AGAPE INSISTS US TO LEAD OTHERS

## Annie Georgekutty RN, MSN-PCSA, DNP

Nurses are expected to provide collaborative care to sick patients to promote health. In addition, as a nurse, I believe treating patients with respect, compassion, and dignity is an important step to show Christ-like character. However, nurses do not get much training and preparation on providing compassionate care but attain this skill when they face emotional circumstances or are challenged by difficult issues.

In a psychiatric hospital, often the patients get admitted at the worst time in their lives. I noticed when patients' maladaptive behavior escalates, frustration of staff members increases. Therefore, instead of providing compassionate care they revert to providing forced care. I decided to change the mannerisms of one of the units by implementing compassionate care. The first step is reinforcing to all staff members expectations to treat their coworkers with respect. Also, I encouraged staff members to maintain their tone when interacting with patients, even in an emergency situation; because a high tone may be misinterpreted by a patient as a 'mean nursing staff'.

While these strategies were being implemented, I met with one of the nurses to address a performance issue. During our meeting, she began to discuss her childhood issues, her upbringing by her parents and the problems she encountered even in her married life, and she unexpectedly burst into tears. Although this nurse was born and brought up in a Christian family, and living as a born-again Christian, things happening around her did not make sense to her. She felt her problems were bigger than she could bear, and no help was available to support her mental health needs. She felt as though Jesus did not hear her prayers. Due to depression and loneliness, she backslid from her faith and stopped going to church for over 30 years. She adopted resilient characteristics to avoid being bullied by others in the community and at work. However, she continued to maintain Christian characteristics by not lying, stealing, or committing adultery.

Romans 15:1 & 2(NKJV) says, "We then who are strong ought to bear with the scruples of the weak, and not to please ourselves. Let each of us please *his* neighbor for *his* good, leading to edification." I spent a few minutes with her, revealing factual challenges people face in their lives. I said to her, "remember everyone will have challenges, and there's no one in this world who does not endure hardship, even when Jesus lived on this earth, he faced many problems." Sometimes we may think Jesus had a special anointing and heavenly protection because HE is the son of God and therefore was able to overcome all the challenges HE faced while HE was on this earth. Don't forget! When Jesus was hanging on the cross, HE was in much pain due to physical injury, and people ridiculed HIM. "He saved others; Himself He cannot save. If He is the King of Israel, let Him now come down from the cross, and we will believe Him." Mathew 27: 42, *NKJV.* Besides, even HIS heavenly father turned his face away from Jesus since HE was carrying the sins of all mankind. Jesus felt a big separation from HIS father. At that time, through the special heavenly anointing Jesus could have jumped off the cross and showed them HE is the true son of God but HE did not. If HE did, HE would have proved HE was equal to a mere mortal man, showing HIS anger and selfishness. So, HE suffered willingly and accepted mocking from others; still pouring out his last drop of blood for mankind, and submitted to the will of HIS father. What a great example of obedience Jesus showed to HIS father." As soon as she heard this, she realized everyone had their own problems, yet she is still loved by Jesus.

A few days later when I met her again, she mentioned she started reading the Bible every day before going to work. Problems still existed in her life but the peace that passes all understanding covered her and she is now able to concentrate on her work better. She is looking to become part of a church again. God taught her that challenges in life can exacerbate anxiety and/or depression.

Therefore, every individual must develop a personal relationship with our Heavenly Father. Even if we backslide from faith, through our personal relationship, the Holy Spirit will remind us, convict us and prevent us from committing sin. So, the first step is developing a trust in the Lord. Our relationship with the Heavenly Father would be greater and nothing else would move us out of His love. As Christians it is important to understand our Lord is a rock and HE is our strong refuge. Even when bad things happen in our lives our God is able to change the situation for our good. We may not be able to change the situation the way we prefer, so why bother pondering over it? It will only increase our anxiety. So let us leave room for God to work. When we put our trust in the Lord willingly and firmly, most mental health issues will have no place in our mind.

After this encounter I realized that through poor work life balance, workplace stress not only causes poor nutrition, tension headaches, cardiovascular issues, and anxiety in healthcare workers, but also exacerbates depression and hatred towards patients and coworkers. Therefore, in order for *nurses to provide compassionate care to patients, nurse leaders should provide compassionate leadership.* Also, a nurse leader must be self-disciplined with a positive demeanor when engaging with others and not intend personal or professional gain. Only then can they contribute to the well-being of the healthcare workers. Thus, a nurse leader can establish success in the professional setting by being transparent in his/her motives.

This incident helped me draw conclusion to the huge need to develop Christian leaders in the healthcare field. I have begun encouraging mission minded youth to specialize in nursing administration because we have a Christian obligation to stop this land from continuing wrong doings leading to increases in mental health issues. Psalms 125:3 (NKJV) says, "For the scepter of wickedness shall not rest on the land allotted to the righteous, lest the righteous reach out their hands to iniquity."

To prevent the righteous generation from doing evil or engaging in sinful activities through different types of addictions, we need to develop and build a community of righteous people. This interaction taught me that a Christian nurse leader plays a vital role in minimizing workplace stress by creating a professional environment exhibiting Christ-like character. This is what the scripture says:

> *"Where there is no counsel, the people fall;*
> *But in the multitude of counselors there is*
> *safety." Proverbs 11: 14, NKJV*

A Christian nurse leader will be able to set practices that enhance the lives of the patients and the nurses in an organization.

# FOURTEEN YEARS AGO

## Benjamin George, MD

Feb 19th 2015. 6:00 PM, a 911 call was made by my niece when she found her Aunt Betty unconscious and unresponsive. EMT was summoned to take Betty from our home. The ambulance arrived quickly and rushed her to Robert Wood Johnson Hospital, New Brunswick, NJ. A massive midbrain bleed kept Betty deeply comatose. She was intubated, ventilated and transferred to the Neuro ICU in an unstable condition. She didn't respond to any treatment and received her last rites on March 2nd 2015. A final call was made to say good bye and send her to be with her Lord and Master: her Creator. I stood beside her ICU bed with full understanding of the Lord's plan in our life knowing her next stop would be to heaven. Betty's life was a blessed one though filled with a myriad of medical problems.

Betty never questioned God's plan. In the midst of unending medical issues she was always satisfied and always having an attitude of praise to the Lord. She found healing in medical problems by divine interventions. That day, standing before the crowd of friends, relatives, and church family I had no words to explain my grief, but was proud to talk about this lady who chose to live with me for 36 years, an IQ of 130, a valedictorian, a state rank holder, a gold medalist in her medical school, an ardent follower of the Lord, with a prayerful attitude always, a counsellor to many, and a problem solver to medical issues nationally and internationally.

But Betty almost went to heaven several years ago....
To be exact, **Fourteen years ago...**

> *"I know a man in Christ who fourteen years ago—whether in the body I do not know, or whether out of the body I do not know, God knows—such a one was caught up to the third heaven."*
> *2 Corinthians 12:2, NKJV*

Feb 19th 2001:
Apt # 42, 10 Amsterdam Ave, New York, NY. 6:00AM

I was ready for work and said goodbye to Betty. Everything was fine as usual. I had rushed that morning to Long Island College Hospital, Brooklyn, NY for work.

At 7:00 AM Betty got up, her usual rising hour, but a little tired. She said to herself "Better I stay at home and sleep a little more". But it was a special today at the department of Endocrinology in St. Lukes Roosevelt Hospital (currently Mount Sinai-St. Luke's Hospital) Betty had an important assignment: to introduce the guest lecturer for the monthly department meeting.

**1111 Amsterdam Ave New York, NY.**

Betty walks to cross the busy Amsterdam Ave to reach St. Lukes Roosevelt hospital. A little while earlier the "fellows" rounds had just finished. At 8:00 AM the endocrinology department opens the meeting for the fellows, residents and medical students. Present were the special guest lecturer, attending physicians, and the chief of the department of endocrinology. Betty got up to introduce the speaker. She narrated to me later, "I got up to present the speaker and as I walked up to the podium, I felt the worst headache drumming up like I've never felt before. It happened so quickly and I then felt dizzy and the next thing I remember is seeing myself on an ICU bed with monitors, a host of doctors, the neurologist Dr. L and our friends".

A call came from Roosevelt Hospital, "Dr. George, Betty is not well and is admitted to the ICU, please come to Roosevelt Hospital". I rushed to Roosevelt Hospital to the Neuro ICU. Dr. L was very kind, understanding and said "It looks like Betty fell down after introducing the speaker sustaining a seizure. The CT scan showed a bleed from a berry aneurysm in the posterior communicating artery at the circle of Willis ". He continued "I gave her a dose of Nifedipine, a calcium channel blocker which should help her. " He tried to reassure me saying "And you know the blood sugars were normal"

"Hello Betty", I said reassuringly. She was able to communicate and as were talking the monitors attached to her were changing in variation. She said "I might need Thiopental!" and soon after her statement she had another seizure. "Oh! She asked for an anticonvulsant knowing it was coming. She is astute and aware of her condition. Her diagnosis has been confirmed. She has a subarachnoid hemorrhage and our options are to coil the bleeding artery or proceed with an open craniotomy to clip the aneurysm. We need the right neuro-surgeon and I think Dr. EF from Beth Israel North Hospital in New York City will be apt for this intervention." Soon she was in the ambulance enroute to Beth Israel North, a short stop away from Roosevelt hospital. Accompanied by a neurologist we arrived at Beth Israel North Hospital. It felt like the longest journey I ever made. Dr. Flam was quick to see her that evening and said "We have a choice of clipping the vessel or an open craniotomy." He discussed all its pros and cons. I sent for our daughter Krupa to come from college saying" Mum has a headache and is admitted in the hospital, do come ASAP" "Well why should I come for a headache?" Krupa retorted. I said firmly "DO COME."

An angiogram was done next to confirm the location of the aneurysm. Dr. B, a well-known interventional radiologist, had a detailed look. A final decision was made by Dr. EF for an emergency craniotomy to clip the aneurysm. There was a long await outside the OR and finally Dr. EF came outside to update me. "Her surgery went well and she should recover, I am sure she is a fighter. As you know 50% of sub-arachnoid hemorrhage (SAH) patients don't even see the hospital at all" Dr. EF tried reassuring me. But post coiling Betty developed all possible complications including vasospasm, ischemia of brain, infection, raised intracranial pressures, VP shunt placement and post operative coma. She went into a coma for three days continuing to be in the ICU intubated and ventilated. We started a prayer vigil around the clock, where friends, relatives and family all over the world started praying. Rev J.D. sat through one night reciting psalms 1 to 150!! Later Betty recalled someone reading Psalms to her although completely comatose at that time and with no response.

12:00 AM Feb. 23rd 2001:

New York City was sleepless as usual and so was I. The neurosurgery ICU was quiet and everyone was asleep except me. Alarms from Betty's monitor continued giving a stable rhythm. Standing beside Betty's bed looking at the monitors, 22 years of our life together rolled into my thoughts. But another dreaded complication set in: post subarachnoid hemorrhage vasospasm. More anxious moments and Betty went into a deep coma. Her blood supply to a major portion of the brain was compromised. The brain doppler didn't look encouraging. We sent prayer requests to her friends, relatives and churches we knew around the world. The ICU team gave a gloomy picture channeling the worst outcome. I didn't lose hope. I consolidated my faith and trust in the Lord, crying to the Lord for His mercies. Evening rounds were over. The ICU team appeared somber, and I knew a reflection of her dismal prognosis. I didn't ask for any clarification. I knew the Lord would take care of her. It was difficult to console my daughter. I had no answer to her questions. I just nodded at her queries. "Benji, leave her alone, let her go, don't make her suffer any more." My friends called and warned me. I didn't have an answer for them.

11:30 PM Feb. 23rd 2001:

Again, here I was, beside her bed, following the monitor screens, looking at Betty's every heartbeat when suddenly the EKG rhythm didn't look normal. It quickly shifted to rapid tachycardia, to ventricular fibrillation and finally to a flat tracing. It was a cardiac arrest! "Ms. Rachel," I shouted for the nurse. "Betty is gone!". Rachel alerted the emergency response system. The following steps happened quickly. I was pushed out by the rapid code team, followed by their execution of a cardiac arrest protocol. From a distance I watched the monitor screen and heard "3...2...1, All clear? Shock!" There was no response for a few moments. Again, 3..2..1, All clear? Shock!" This time the rhythm changed and a normal EKG was displayed on the screen. I said "Thank God!" thinking she had almost gone away to her maker. However, she was back but continued to be in a coma.

My mind was going through emotional cycles. I questioned the Lord...Why me? Why did Betty go through this ordeal? Is there no way out? No solutions? Her future looked bleak. My friends, relatives, and pastors all tried to console me. Betty's departmental chief outlined the challenges and he was not alone. Several proclaimed her grave prognosis. My daughter Krupa was a great friend during this challenging time. Ruby, Betty's sister tried to empathize but nothing worked to console me.

I continued to question the Lord, trying to hold on to her and bring her back to life. Three days later, my father's close friend came to visit and pray for Betty. I didn't know him personally but the Lord had a specific plan through him with a message of salvation. He didn't talk much. He told me: "Stop holding on to Betty...leave her to the Lord..." He started praying in no uncertain terms, with complete hope and confidence. I felt heaven coming down and touching my heart. I had never heard such an authoritative prayer before. I said, "Amen" as he finished and he left quietly with no comments. I never met him again but he left a lasting image of Christ's love and compassion in my heart.

I prayed: "Thank you Lord for Betty's life. You gave her to me. She is yours. She is your daughter, I commit her to you. Take her and I have no complaints. Whatever happens You are in charge. Praise the Lord..." I felt a great sigh of relief; a peace like never before. The creator of the universe standing before a puny me with a message of salvation. My eyes were wet and my heart was pounding. I don't remember how long I stood in that position. As minutes passed Betty's eyes were fluttering and she opened her eyes; she made some noise. She became conscious but couldn't say a word, she was aphasic and paralyzed on the right side. But this response was reassuring and strengthened me. Gradually, after several days, she was weaned off the ventilator and extubated. She was uncommunicative at first but her speech gradually improved. She said "I made a trip to the heavens, a place where streets are really gold, colors are perfect, red is red, gold is golden, blue is perfect. I met my perfectly healthy mother among the angelic choir..." Three weeks later Betty walked home, improved in speech but mildly weak on the right side. Three months later her neurologist asked, "Which side was she paralyzed? I find no deficits between your right and left!"

Betty went back to active medical practice and was a

consolation to many. The SAH complications left Betty with uncontrolled diabetes mellitus, salt wasting nephropathy, seizures, coronary artery disease, multiple angioplasties and many others. But she found complete healing from the Lord in all those situations. The spiritual healing and blessings she experienced after these events turned out to be a blessing for our family.

Now, even though, Betty has joined the heavenly choir, she stands out as a blessing and an assurance that the Lord is real and His blessings are eternal. "Bless the Lord, oh my soul and all that is within me, bless His holy name. Bless the Lord, O my soul, and forget not all His benefits...."

# ARE YOU BLIND ENOUGH TO SEE OR SIGHTED ENOUGH TO BE BLIND?

## Minu Mathew George, MD

As healthcare workers, we are given the privilege to touch the lives of many around us every day. Our patients and families are thankful and reach out to share their gratitude in many ways. They may send notes, fill out recognition cards, respond to patient experience surveys or fill out google reviews. Often in healthcare we incorrectly think clinicians are the only ones making an impact. One of my patients reversed this assumption being "blind enough to see" and profoundly impacted me as a clinician by touching my personal Christian walk.

Being born blind with Optic Nerve Hypoplasia, an inability to see like blind Bartimaeus of the Scriptures, is a lifelong sentence in darkness, or so I thought. An inability to enjoy the colors as the leaves turn colors in the fall or the beautiful blooms of the spring or the ability to live life to the fullest. Endocrinologists see many patients affected with pituitary hormone deficiency where a lifelong hormone replacement adds to the disease burden. Nevertheless, this particular person with septo-optic dysplasia (SOD) left an imprint upon me changing my perspective forever.

It was early in my career, when I was filled with self-doubt, the well-known imposter syndrome and various other stressors coming in between learning a new specialty; life was filled with worries and uncertainties. However, every time this blind patient came in, he was filled with much hope and the joy of the Lord. Due to his blindness; his other senses were heightened. He played music masterfully and belted out beautiful melodious hymns and songs in perfect form. With his free time, he listened to the audio Bible, memorizing scriptures and putting together amazing sermons with the help of the Holy Spirit. He became a minister while still a teenager. Every time he was on my schedule to adjust his medications, I looked forward to that encounter with him. He would sing a song for me, tell me about his preaching schedule and tell me about what the Lord was teaching him. Such amazing insights, zeal for the Lord and His ministry was evident every time he came for his appointment. He became an inspiration for me to do all I could in helping and ministering to others in my life.

In John Chapter 9 we see a man born blind at birth. Jesus said "this happened so that the power of God could be seen in him" . The Pharisees could not agree and refused to believe in Jesus but this man testified "I was blind and now I can see!" In 9:37-39 (NKJV) " Jesus said to him, "you have both seen Him and it is He who is talking with you." Then he said, "Lord, I believe!" And he worshiped Him. And Jesus said, "for judgment I have come into this world, that those who do not see may see, and that those who see may be made blind." My patient was also blind enough to see fully! This young man serves as an inspiration for me and he has touched my life with the power of God evident in his life.

# CALLED TO BE
# DILIGENT INNKEEPERS

## Sebin George, MD

Though it was a busy morning at the community hospital's pediatric OPD (out-patient department), Master J's family stood out from the crowd, mostly due to their distressed faces. After spending a few months in the hospital, it was easier to identify those coming from Jawadhi hills, an area predominantly inhabited by tribal communities – they often looked confused, and their children were brought to the hospital only after extreme sickness. The delay was due to multiple reasons, including poverty and poor access to health being some of the barriers. An initial assessment revealed he had been unwell for about three weeks and with significant weight loss. Since he needed a detailed evaluation, he was referred to the medical college town campus where the community health department belonged.

As the institution had a policy to support their work in the tribal community, the family's inability to pay did not hinder the referral process. He was treated nearly free of cost and discharged after being pronounced fever-less for a few days. Unexpectedly, his condition deteriorated a few days after his discharge. A doctor from our department who visited the child's village saw him extremely sick and advised his parents to bring him back to the hospital as soon as possible. Although he had demonstrated considerable improvement after treatment, his deterioration made us wonder in retrospect if he should have been transferred back to the community hospital for a few days of observation before being sent home, considering the distance and difficulty in accessing healthcare. While this was certainly a gap we needed to address, the urgent matter currently was his stabilization and re-admission. Though such a decision regarding hospitalization may seem straightforward to many readers, those accustomed to the way of rural life and tribal communities may appreciate the complexity of decision-making and the stakeholders contributing to it.

The day he was seen by the doctor was on the 'Amavasya' – the lunar phase of the new moon, the day considered auspicious for the worship of forefathers' spirits. Elders in the village forbade the family from sending him to the hospital on 'Amavasya', as they believed he was unlikely to return home alive if he left the village on that particular day. Despite multiple pleas by the doctor, the decision remained unchanged, and he was brought to the hospital only the following day. By then, he had multiple convulsions and was in a drowsy state. After initial stabilization, he was referred to the tertiary care hospital, where he required mechanical ventilation, being unable to maintain a regular breathing pattern. He remained in the pediatric ICU for a month, the treating team not leaving any stone unturned in arriving at a diagnosis. He even required a bedside surgical procedure to relieve the pressure building up inside his brain. Despite various investigations and multidisciplinary team meetings, Master J's diagnosis remained elusive, yet he began to improve slowly. Once he was weaned off oxygen support and stabilized, he was transported to the community hospital for nutritional rehabilitation and physiotherapy exercises.

He was emaciated and unresponsive when he returned to us, as his sensorium was abnormal and he was being fed via a tube inserted into the stomach through his nose. We taught his mother simple measures such as frequent position changes to avoid pressure ulcers, chest physiotherapy to prevent lung infections, and feeding via nasogastric tube. Our physiotherapist was instrumental in teaching her passive muscle-stretching exercises, and in arranging a special mattress to prevent excessive pressure over his bony prominences. His mother was extremely faithful in following instructions and the most efficient member caring for Master J. While we were happy to see his improvement- he began to verbalize, obeying simple commands and ate by himself. We remained apprehensive about his long-term outcome and the family's ability to care for him in the village, once he was discharged from the hospital. After reinforcing the home care program with his parents and confirming their readiness to care for him at home, we planned his discharge. Hence, Master J returned to his village after a long seven-week hospital stay, the longest he ever spent away from his home!

As our physiotherapist visited the Community Health Centre at Jawadhi hills a couple of weeks later, the family was asked to bring him for a review, and behold! Master J walked into the clinic without any support and attempted to speak words. This was nothing short of a miracle; a boy who not only lived despite odds but was inching back to normalcy, faster than we had hoped for. Here he was, a common bush, afire with God's mercy, a brother in need, who gave us the privilege of taking care of him and seeing him recover, even when we did not have a definitive diagnosis for him. All of us caring for him had the immense satisfaction of witnessing the joy of a family who received their son back. I felt we merely provided him and his family a shelter to recover and support, while God was healing him.

In the parable of the good samaritan, the innkeeper remains a nameless person; the parable does not focus on him or make him the central character. Nevertheless, it was evident the good samaritan trusted the innkeeper to take care of the wounded man. The gospel does not mention any special character attribute or extraordinary talent he possessed; yet he was entrusted to take care of a fellow human being. Likewise, we have been invited to participate in a health ministry, not to feel sacrificial or to bring glory or attention to ourselves, but to fulfill our roles. Someone once said, we have been called to "do ordinary things with extraordinary love". Truly, it is a great privilege to participate in such poignant journeys, like that of Master J and his family, when people are vulnerable and yet, empowered by love. It is a privilege to be present, so they lean on you, and you, in turn, lean on the 'Rock that is higher than I'.

> *Luke 10: 35, NKJV- "On the next day, when he departed, he took out two denarii, gave them to the innkeeper, and said to him, 'Take care of him; and whatever more you spend, when I come again, I will repay you."*

# A HEALING PSALM

## Tony George, DO

*"The Lord is my Shepherd; I shall not want"*
*-Psalm 23:1, NKJV*

*"To find health should be the object of the
doctor, anyone can find disease"*
*-Andrew Taylor Still MD, DO*

Clerkships are important transitionary points in a student's journey. A third-year medical student goes through rotations in medicine, pediatrics, psychiatry, surgery, obstetrics and gynecology. These core rotations establish their clinical foundation. Long twelve-hour shifts are common where treating the body is emphasized. Students are graded on their diagnostic acumen and their ability to establish rapport, empathy and connection with patients. In a hospital, treating the body and the mind are important. It forms the basis for patient satisfaction through their experience and to a hospital's reputation. Patient recommendations to a relative/friend influences their selection and in turn it impacts hospital revenue and growth. Treating the body and mind was routine; healing the spirit was not, and it was in fact, odd. No medical school graded a student's ability to connect with a person's soul. I was aware of spirit filled anointings and transformative processionals in church but reviving the spirit in a hospital was unusual. I often wondered "how can a physician treat the spirit?" As a Christian physician, I felt I should be inclined and have an answer to this concern. I thought praying would help and I saw physicians pray for their patients. However, I felt I was infringing their privacy and felt uncomfortable initiating a spiritual dialogue. These patients trusted their life-long primary care physicians but why should they trust me through this brief hospital encounter? Early in my rotations, ministering to the spirit often crossed my mind but it faded through the emphasis of managing body and mind. I continued to heal the body and mind putting the spirit behind me.

However, an encounter changed my perspective during my intensive care rotation (ICU) as a fourth-year medical student in York, PA. It was an opportunity to heal the spirit. This appointment was unusual. No preparation was necessary and it did not need a logical explanation. It was not for physical healing, although my patient came physically broken, and it was not for emotional healing, although my patient was in mental anguish.

Every day during my ICU rotation I managed a few patients, evaluating them and writing SOAP notes after my encounters. SOAP notes are clinical snapshots of a patients' progress, with a physicians' examination and a formulation of next steps. ICUs in general have scary reputations with some studies showing 1 in 5 patients die in the ICU. Once in the ICU, patients either improve and move to a step-down unit, or worsen, deteriorate and unfortunately die. Events occurred quickly: either rapid recovery or quick demise.

That morning I visited my new patient, transferred overnight from a nursing home. She was a 78-year-old semi delirious woman with dementia, atrial fibrillation and a rapid ventricular rate. Atrial fibrillation is a heart condition where a regular heartbeat becomes irregular. I walked in, introduced myself as a fourth-year medical student and inquired about her condition. I noticed she was trembling. Being naïve and an amateur, I become anxious and impulsive. Surprisingly her vitals were normal; she was hemo-dynamically stable and there were no immediate concerns of declining health status. I began looking for more clues. I moved to the physical examination by listening to her heart and lungs. Did she agree? I do not know, but I proceeded anyway. I steadied my hand against her trembling, frail body while listening to her heart with my stethoscope. Within two seconds, she was reciting some words. Her sounds came audibly loud through my stethoscope; my ears were uncomfortable. Unable to listen to her heart, I pulled my stethoscope and waited till she was done reciting. Through her weak soft voice, her words and phrases sounded sweetly familiar. Now more audible, she was reciting Psalm 23, *"The Lord is my shepherd; I shall not be in want; he makes me lie down in green pastures, He..."* She stopped, trembling through her recital. She tried again *"The Lord is my shepherd; I shall not be in want; he makes me lie down in green pastures, He..."* She stopped again. She had forgotten the next verse. She backtracked trying to remember and continue her recitation. She persisted but was unable to continue.

She was terrified of her situation, of me, of what would happen next. Here was my moment! I realized I needed to intervene. It was a chosen moment; I didn't have to be summoned; I was appointed for this intervention.

I remembered the Psalm continuing where she had stopped and we finished it together. She looked up at me, her heart consoled, and smiled. We had just finished reciting the whole Psalm together. She was not trembling, her heart beat slowed down, she was calm. I put my stethoscope on her heart and noticed her heart rate had normalized. I thanked her for allowing me to examine her and left the room.

I began to complete my SOAP note recalling this unusual encounter. It felt different, bizarre, but satisfying. It was different from my daily encounters. There was completeness in it and it cured my patient. It didn't require medicines but a narration of scriptures. It was physical, mental and yes, "spiritual". What transpired was a spiritual treatment. A coincidence maybe to some, but to others a purposeful assignment at that particular time. I was thankful for this opportunity to experience this spiritual treatment.

In a few days, my patient left the ICU happy, energetic, and vigorous despite her frail state. Her rhythm reverted to a normal sinus rhythm. Her dementia continued to afflict but she didn't care. I was content knowing I just needed to be present for Him and God would unravel the opportunity himself. God would use me to respond to the needs of the body, mind, and spirit in His time.

# WHEN MEDICAL
# MEETS LEGAL

## Anonymous, MD

As physicians, we are sworn by the Hippocratic oath to do no harm. This means constantly evaluating and assessing every medical decision, whether a particular procedure or treatment will increase the risk of injury to a patient. While the constant mental scrutiny of every medical decision has been ingrained in us since medical school, another aspect of medical practice is hushed for most of our training and career. Most physicians embark on this training only when they meet these situations head-on. This is the impact of medical malpractice.

My first encounter with medical malpractice was during residency training in a critical care setting. I was taken aback when I received an email from my hospital's risk and claims department. This was a department I had never interacted with previously, but I knew their role in medical malpractice. Anxiety began as I read the brief, ominous email requesting a callback. During this conversation, they informed me I was named in a medical practice claim for a patient whose care I was briefly involved in. I recalled the patient and family as they provided the patient's details.

During residency, medical decision-making is led by the attending, who dictates most patient care. Residents have limited independent decision-making authority during this time of training. So, I was surprised I was named in this medical malpractice claim. As I inquired about this, the office informed me that in medical malpractice claims, the entire team is named in the initial filing, given the statute of limitation. The statute of limitations is a law setting the maximum time parties can initiate legal proceedings from the date of an alleged offense. I was learning these medical-legal terminologies for the first time in my career. No one had explained during my medical training what protocol to follow in this situation. There were millions of questions in my head, and there was no roadmap on how to deal with the emotions of this situation. My lawyers advised me not to discuss the case details with colleagues, family, or friends. If I did, they might have to testify if the case went to trial. Their interpretation/ recollection could be used in the case against me. Here you are, dealing with an uncharted situation, anxious and emotionally overwhelmed by its impact on your financial future and reputation. Yet, you cannot talk to anyone about the patient's details except your legal team.

The said patient had not been to a doctor for most of their adult life. He had not been feeling well for many weeks before presenting to the hospital. Despite his symptoms, he did not seek medical attention. He was enjoying a meal at home when he suddenly lost consciousness. His wife called EMS (Emergency Medical Services), and when they arrived, he was found to be in cardiac arrest. They started resuscitation procedures and transferred him to the nearest hospital. With that initial care, he regained consciousness and could communicate with his family. He was evaluated by cardiology, and a cardiac catheterization revealed multiple blockages in his coronary arteries, for which cardiac bypass surgery was recommended. Throughout his hospital stay, he continued to improve. He was diagnosed with many medical problems, given years of no medical follow-up or treatments. The cardiac surgery team began the workup for doing heart surgery while he was in the hospital. However, while he was awaiting surgery, he had another cardiac arrest in the hospital. This time, despite attempts at resuscitation, he never woke up. He deteriorated rapidly and passed away in a few days.

The family, distraught over the turn of events, felt negligence led to his untimely death rather than poor medical follow-up and a compounding of undiagnosed health problems. So, his wife filed a malpractice claim naming the physicians involved in his care. Medical malpractice is defined as any act of commission or omission by a physician during the treatment of a patient that deviates from accepted norms of practice in the medical community, causing an injury to the patient. Over the next few months and years, I had several meetings with lawyers. I learned about the legal proceedings of a medical practice case while living through one. My legal team was very supportive and helped me navigate through the different aspects of this situation. However, being restricted from discussing this highly stressful situation with my family was emotionally very strenuous. Every licensing application asks, "Are you currently named in a malpractice claim?" I had to communicate with my legal team to draft an appropriate answer to that question. I had to provide information about this claim for loan applications. I was denied personal loans because a successful malpractice claim could have purported effects on my financial ability to carry a loan. This ordeal went on for years without communication about this case, to the point you sometimes forgot about its existence. But then it would come back with intensity sucking me back into this vacuum of uncertainty, despair, and hopelessness.

During this time, I relied on prayer and the word. It was a time of trial where I surrendered every aspect of the case and my future to God. As the Bible says in Luke 12:7, *NIV* - "Indeed, the very hairs of your head are all numbered." I had to remind myself that God is in control constantly and is aware of all aspects of the situation.

As years passed, my legal team had me prepare multiple documents regarding my role in this case. The expert witnesses retained by my legal team to review the case also could not find anything erroneous in the care of this patient. The legal team was surprised this case continued despite the lack of specific errors that anyone could ascertain. The plaintiff's legal team attempted to pinpoint different minutiae to substantiate the reason for the patient's death. When we provided a rebuttal, they would return, citing another detail of the case that had no relevance to the patient's outcome. The constant back and forth was very frustrating. I questioned God, why me, and why there was no end in sight? I could not find a specific error that could justify that I deserved this. During this whole time, I lived my personal and professional life pretending this did not exist. Meanwhile, inside my mind, this was a continual source of stress. I could not discuss the case with my colleagues involved in the patient's care. Everyone had their separate legal representation. Each defendant was on their own.

Finally, after almost a decade since my first encounter with the patient, the court dismissed the case. God gave the legal team the wisdom to pursue an avenue they had not considered. They were not optimistic it would work. They asked me to block time in the upcoming months for the trial. But to everyone's surprise, the court ruled in our favor and dismissed the case. This was an unusual outcome atypical for medical malpractice cases. I believe it was God's favor that finally turned the direction of the case around.

Even though the agony is finally over, the emotional scars of this encounter linger. My medical training had taught me to focus on doing no harm to patients, but this experience influenced me to evaluate medical decisions from a legal perspective. As physicians, we constantly deal with unrealistic human expectations and emotions. This can result in patients lashing out at physicians with unsubstantiated complaints. However, there are situations where medical errors are made due to the recklessness of the medical professional, requiring exploration and legal action. However, frivolous lawsuits continue to plague clinicians, and by chance, I was entangled in one early in my career. I thank God for His recourse. As I continue this journey to provide the best possible care for my patients, I ask God for wisdom for every patient encounter and medical decision.

# ICU in the Bush

## Mandy Glass & Diana Zwijnenburg, MD

*Jeroen and Diana Zwijnenburg have served with MAF (Mission Aviation Fellowship) in Papua New Guinea since 2021, with Jeroen as Projects & Finance Manager and Diana as a doctor at Kompian Hospital.*

*In this story, Diana shares the challenges of saving someone's life in the bush with limited resources, how the nurses and the patient's family saw the medical process, and using a homemade ICU.*

The call came on a Friday morning. It was a typical bright and sunny day, and a medical evacuation (Medevac) flight was requested from a remote village to our hospital, a 12-minute flight over rugged terrain, which would take at least two full days by foot. If you're fit, that is. Earlier that day, a man, Nepo, was working under his house, and the roof collapsed on top of him; he was pulled from under the rubble and badly injured. Fortunately, he was the only one injured.

The local community health worker (CHW) informed us that Nepo had a broken leg, maybe a broken pelvis, and was crying in pain. What else was injured was challenging to assess. We instructed the CHW to administer morphine and triggered the request for a medevac with MAF.

MAF responded quickly, but the plane was busy working in another province. A few hours later, the aircraft became free and headed to pick up our patient. It was almost 5 pm when the patient arrived. Nepo was in his late forties, wrapped in mosquito net and other clothes to carry him into the plane. Upon landing, he was barely responsive, and together with a group of men, we pulled him onto our spinal board and carried him to our ambulance for the short ride from the airstrip to the hospital.

On initial assessment, though barely conscious, he was breathing ok; however, I was concerned about signs of a base skull fracture with blood coming out from his ear. His right upper leg was broken, and there was a nasty graze with developing bruising across the front of his chest. Other than these, he seemed ok.

Our X-ray machine was broken, but we had an ultrasound machine, which was a real blessing. It showed there were no collapsed lungs or blood in his abdomen or pelvis, so I was reasonably confident there was no major pelvic fracture.

Then, there was the concern of protecting his neck, which is a standard measure in all trauma cases. I had no X-ray to check, but with reduced consciousness and a distracting leg fracture, his neck could not be cleared, anyway. However, his head had been wobbling unprotected from the time of the accident until now, and he was still able to move all limbs. Should I put him in an ill-fitting collar, potentially increasing the pressure in his head and making the potential skull base fracture worse? I left the neck, assuming it was uninjured.

We took blood to check his blood count and group and got the theatre girls to fit a traction pin. Under mild sedation and local anesthetics, I inserted a traction pin in his lower leg and hung some weights on it. This instantly made his broken leg look straighter.

The next day, Nepo looked better. He was now fully conscious, suggesting that his mild head injury, together with the morphine he was given, was a plausible explanation for his drowsiness the day before. He was clinically stable and oriented but he did not remember what had happened. His leg pain was manageable, and he was in good spirits. Bit by bit, we were able to get the whole story.

These stones were quite large, and falling from a height of 2 meters, they could cause significant damage, making me worry about his chest. I examined him again but could not find any broken ribs. Then I discussed with the hospital staff that if his story is true, his condition could deteriorate a lot over the next 1-2 days due to lung bruising.

We did not have to wait long. By the following day, Nepo needed oxygen nasal prongs, and over the following 24 hours, he deteriorated further. By Monday morning, he was on dual oxygen, and when we finished our usual rounds to check on him again, he was working hard, the double source oxygen keeping his saturation level around 60-70% (which should be 100%). It was going to be only another few hours before his demise. We needed to intubate him and put him on a ventilator until his lungs healed enough to breathe again on his own. This is would be a straightforward decision in most hospitals in developed countries. But here, in the middle of nowhere, with few resources and inexperienced staff, it was a different battle. However, without much time to think, I spoke to the family on imminent steps, who agreed, although I felt they would agree to anything to prevent this man from dying.

I got our equipment together. I had a simple oxygen-powered ventilator, intubation equipment, a suction machine from the labor ward, and various drugs I needed. I was blessed with two competent junior doctors and an HEO (Health Extension Officer) at my side, who were willing to help even though this situation was outside their comfort zone. By now, the man was on his last few breaths, bathing in sweat from his breathing effort; he could barely manage a saturation of 50%.

But first, we prayed. We prayed that the God of heaven and earth, the maker and sustainer of all life, would help us this day. We prayed for peace for the family and a smooth intubation. We prayed for Nepo to live, for God to give him a second chance at life so that he could glorify His holy name.

Then we went ahead. Positioned the patient, pushed the drugs, waited for it to work, and inserted the breathing tube. A large audience of staff, patients, and caregivers watched. It went well, and his saturation rose to over 95% within a few minutes. Everyone breathed a sigh of relief. I secured the tube, listened to either side to make sure it was secured well, connected it to the little ventilator, took care of straps not cutting into his skin, and taped his eyes shut. I then administered some sedatives to keep him asleep.

The monitoring had come off due to the patient's old monitoring pads and sweat. So, we sponged and cleaned him, put a new clean sheet on the bed, and reattached the monitoring. Everything went smoothly until now, but I needed to prepare for what was coming next. The family had moved away and were now looking from a distance. Any attempt to involve them was futile. It was clear they would not come near or touch their relative.

While I had everyone's attention, I discussed the importance of nursing support to always be with this man. Nepo needed to be watched regardless of lunchtime, breaks, or other jobs. Then I realized most of them had no clue what to watch out for or do in case of a problem. Then, I discussed suctioning. Every hour, the tube needed to be suctioned. More blank faces. Mouth care, eye care, turning/skin care, NG tube feeds, alarms, the pump, and monitor values to alert a doctor. My staff had not seen before, let alone done before, but in typical Melanesian fashion, they nodded and said yes, indicating their willingness. Still, I knew nothing would be done the way I had explained unless I showed them first and we did it together.

So, we did: with each new staff changeover, explaining repeatedly, ensuring they knew how to look after this man. In the meantime, I was trying to get my medication cocktail correctly in the syringe. In an ICU setting, many medications are given through different syringes and pumps, which can be adjusted to the patient's needs. We, however, had one pump, so it all had to go into one syringe.

The first few days went well, but we quickly realized we would run out of oxygen bottles before the weekend.

We usually get new bottles supplied, but the road to the provincial capital was still blocked after the election violence. A hospital car had been allowed to pass, but the situation was tense, and the Kompiam drivers were not keen to go. This was one of many things the hospital needed. We ran out of almost everything, including bandages, gauze, and various medications. So, a vehicle had to go, and after much hesitation, two drivers went and switched over the empty oxygen bottles for full ones and picked up some supplies for the pharmacy. They came back safely, and everyone was relieved when they were back and almost cheered when they entered the hospital gate on their return.

In the meantime, I ran out of some medications, and constantly needed to change the contents of the syringe due to some drugs not working, working unreliably (most of our drugs are 5-10 years out of date), or being out of stock. This and the continuous supervising of most of his care became very tiring. One night, I found both night nurses asleep, with nobody watching the patient, which was quickly rectified and did not happen again. Nepo also had developed some pressure sores, likely because he was not being turned every 2 hours. We took care of dressing his wounds and turning him frequently to prevent deterioration.

All this time, the family kept their distance. Gradually, their fears were verbalized: they had been terrified. They were sure that this was all caused by an evil spirit, likely the spirit of the first husband of this man's second wife. They blamed this spirit for letting the house collapse and were afraid it would bring more trouble. They also did not know what happened to the patient's spirit, as he was lying still in the bed, apart from some coughing when being suctioned. It was heartbreaking to see the magnitude of fear that had accumulated in the people's minds. Our local pastor came and spoke to the people in their language. Then we prayed because our God was greater than all these spirits and fears.

I decided to try to extubate him on the 5th day. His airway pressures were reasonable, and all his numbers were looking good. Also, there was not much debris anymore when suctioning. So, we got our equipment ready again for potential reintubation and stopped the sedation. Then we waited, and for about three hours, we stood there, and not much happened. The patient started to breathe again, feebly and certainly not enough to support himself. Three hours of waiting was enough. All these drugs, with their unpredictable actions, very likely had accumulated and were not helping. Besides, the people in PNG are more sensitive to some of the medicines. I admitted defeat, put him back on the ventilator, and started a different (much shorter acting) sedative, thinking let's try again in a day or two. Weaning off a ventilator is gradual when the ventilator recognizes the patient's breathing and synchronizes the breaths given. In this case, most medication can already be reduced before removing the breathing tube. But our little ventilator was unable to do this, so it was all or nothing, and I had to keep him in a deeper sleep so he would tolerate the ventilator. The downside of this different sedative was the dose in the syringe finished much quicker. This meant that it needed to be changed every 4 hours, regardless of whether it was day or night.

Another two days went by, and I decided to try again. We repeated this setup with all the equipment we had prepared earlier. We prayed again, leaving it all in God's hands, the only Healer, the mighty God and Lord of heaven and earth, supreme over all spirits. Then the syringe stopped, I suctioned all the debris, and the patient coughed up and started breathing stronger. The ventilator was stopped, and oxygen was connected to the end of the tube. Initially, saturations dropped to 50% but slowly increased to 60% and 70%, then with coughing down to 50%, but quickly back up, now to 80%. Over time, it gradually improved, and I took the breathing tube out. Nepo was now on his own. We put on concentrated oxygen, made sure he sat up as much as he could tolerate, and waited. The next hour would be crucial. Would his energy sustain his breathing? His lungs were still stiff, and it would take effort to overcome. Gradually, we saw his breathing rate decrease and his effort normalize without his saturation dropping. He was successfully extubated. God had done it!

The family now approached a little closer. Two hours later, Nepo opened his eyes for the first time since several days after a family member called his name. This was also the first time the family was standing around his bed again.

From here on, Nepo improved quickly. Initially confused, he managed to stand on his good leg, wondering why we had tied his other leg to the bed. He was reminded again his leg was broken and kept in traction. This time, the family, who moved closer, were very much involved in his day-to-day care. We took his feeding tube out, and he began to eat and drink. For a while, he was still in hospital, waiting for his leg to heal. Soon, his traction would be removed so he could get out again. We prayed for this man and his family. We prayed for the Holy Spirit to fill their hearts so that they would glorify their maker and sustainer and would not be afraid of other spirits. We prayed that everyone involved would see God's hand in this through His healing power. We prayed for the people of PNG to find salvation in Jesus so His name would be lifted.

After about two months of therapy, Nepo was finally discharged from the hospital. The only way to get back to Pyarulama was again by MAF aircraft. Recovering from his lagging fracture, he could not hike back, which takes 2-3 days if someone is fit and healthy. The flight coincided with a team from the Kompiam Hospital going out for their quarterly patrol to Pyarulama. Nepo and another discharged patient with a foot injury shared the back seat of the aircraft, happy to be homebound again.

For the patrol team, who knew Nepo, it was remarkable to witness his reception upon his return. Rachael Hopkins, recently joining as a Junior Doctor from the UK, shared, "It was so special to witness his return home. Everyone was gathering around and crying."

# THERE NEEDS TO BE JUSTICE

## Mandy Glass, MD

*Zechariah 7:9, NKJV- "Thus says the LORD of hosts: 'Execute true justice, show mercy and compassion, everyone to his brother."*

As I prepared the stretcher for our medevac patient, I overheard snippets of the story... "Young girl... raped by two men... if she dies, we will kill them..." were the words of the pilot as she shared the tragic scene with me.

"The reality sunk in as the girl was carried and laid on the stretcher on the ground next to our aircraft," the pilot added.

In remote Papua New Guinea (PNG), small aircraft function as ambulances, flying patients who otherwise would have to be hand-carried for hours, if not several days, across high mountains, steep valleys, or large swamps to hospitals where professional medical care is still basic but often life-saving. Facilitating medical evacuation flights (medevacs) is a tough task for our pilots as they see the (injured) patients and learn about the condition requiring medical care at a hospital, even more so if the patient is a victim of sexual abuse. Our pilots must focus on delivering a safe flight operation in one of the world's most challenging environments.

The pilot continued to share with her what happened at the airstrip.

"I crouched down next to the girl to try and reassure her ahead of the flight. Eyes full of emptiness looked back at me. Would this young girl ever smile again after what had happened to her? Would this plane trip to the hospital only add to her nightmares?"

The flight was launched earlier that day and offered a training opportunity for my team colleague to observe one of our most experienced pilots responding to a medevac call for a 10-year-old girl who was the victim of a vicious sexual assault.

While the pilot in command prepared the cabin and paperwork for taking the girl to the hospital, the trainee pilot located the parents in a group of bystanders.

"I learned that the girl had been raped at night, already some time ago," she recalled. "The men were not from this village. Meanwhile, two perpetrators had been caught and were held in custody, but two others were still on the run."

These are tough conversations to have under the wing of an aircraft. Pilots normally don't have the time and peace of mind to engage in such a personal and, in this case, intimate way with their medevac passengers. Being an observer pilot and being a young woman meant that my friend had the capacity to share a few words of comfort with the girl and her family using the local trade language of Tok Pisin.

"As I looked at the girl lying on the stretcher, I could not fathom how anyone could do such a thing to an innocent child. She kept on staring blankly into space. 'Mi sori tru,' I told her parents (I'm really sorry). I didn't have the words to say how heartbroken I was for her and them. All I could do was to hope that they knew," she said.

Meanwhile, the experienced pilot communicated with the local MAF agent and the health worker, surrounded by many people from the community. Everyone knew that the girl would receive treatment in the hospital, but would she receive justice?

"They try to save the life of the little child, the MAF agent told me, which is why they want the child to be flown to the hospital," the pilot said. "If the girl does not survive, there will be compensation claims in the normal PNG way. If the girl does survive, the perpetrators might get away with it, and that's not good. There needs to be justice!"

When details emerged later from the hospital, it revealed that Esther (not her real name) had struggled to speak out about the rape.

"Esther is a 10-year-old girl from a very remote village who was admitted to our hospital and flown in by MAF. She is a Grade 2 student in the local village school. According to her parents, she had been generally unwell for about three months with intermittent episodes of vomiting, fevers, poor appetite, and generalized body weakness. She did not tell her parents about the incident due to fear of being punished or beaten up by her parents," the residential medical officer (RMO) of the hospital said.

"One day, whilst walking to the garden with her older

sister, she fainted and, upon persistent questioning, told her sister what happened to her. She finally told the parents that she had been assaulted by two men known to them. These men were their own 'wantoks' (relatives) living with them and cared for by her parents.

"By the time of discovery, they no longer lived under the same roof. Her father was furious and wanted to take matters into his own hands, but the alleged perpetrators were no longer in the village. The parents decided to report the matter to the local community leaders and to bring her to the district hospital for assessment and treatment.

"At the hospital, we diagnosed Esther with malaria and treated her accordingly. However, due to the late presentation, any physical evidence of her attack would be difficult to attain; and a physical examination would likely cause psychological stress to her without yielding many useful findings. Her parents have been informed of this."

"Her parents still want the two alleged perpetrators brought to justice. They plan to bring their case to the police with the community's support once she gets discharged from the hospital," the RMO said. The Superintendent of the District Hospital concurred with the pilot's assessment that it was unlikely the girl would receive justice.

"With the village being so far away also, it is very likely that this issue will get resolved at the village with either compensation or revenge - and no true justice for the affected child. I suppose ultimately only God can bring that. A very sad story," she said.

For many victims like Esther, shame, and fear will cover up a lot of these crimes, not only in the remote villages of Papua New Guinea but worldwide, especially in societies where men hold the power and culture allows for it.

However, there's one who will wash away all tears and restore peace. Peace of heart, peace of mind, and peace of mankind. He is the one who has promised that "God will wipe away every tear from their eyes; there shall be no more death, nor sorrow, nor crying. There shall be no more pain, for the former things have passed away." Revelation 21:4, *NKJV*

That's when Esther, too, will get justice.

# CYTOGENETICS

## Milly James, CG(ASCP)<sup>CM</sup>

The characters and circumstances in the following story are fictional. However, the cytogenetic methods, processes, and tools are real and used daily in a modern cytogenetics lab. The story illustrates how they are used together to provide a proper and correct diagnosis.

Sara McConnell had never imagined her career could impact the lives of many people. Growing up, Sara wanted to be in the medical field to interact with patients and to help them. She had been fascinated by the intricate world of genetics. Her passions led her to a career as a Cytogenetics Technologist and brought her to the cutting edge of medical science. She would see many cases and had an opportunity to empathize with the patients and pray over each case. Every day, she worked with genetic analysis tools like FISH, karyotyping, and microarray to unravel the mysteries hidden within the chromosomes of her patients. Today was no different as she had to face a very challenging case.

Emily, Sara's manager, received an emergency phone call from the Pediatric Department at Emmanuel Children's

Hospital located in the heart of the city. Emmanuel Hospital was not far from Fair Haven University Cytogenetics Lab, where Emily and Sara worked. Dr. Rodriguez, the head of the Pediatric Department, told Emily they were sending a 5-year-old boy's blood sample. Dr. Rodriguez suspected the patient may have Leukemia and prioritized the case as STAT to prepare for a treatment plan if needed. In the Cytogenetics Lab, STAT cases were treated with the highest priority, with results turned around within 4 hours. Emily urgently messaged Sara, in charge of FISH (Fluorescence In Situ Hybridization), to prioritize this case as STAT until the results were sent out. Sara knew every minute counted when a young patient's health was at stake. The hospital courier soon delivered the STAT case – a 5ml sodium heparin tube with the blood sample. Sodium heparin tubes are ideal to avoid any blood coagulation. Emily specifically instructed Dr. Rodriguez to collect the sample in a sodium heparin tube so results could be provided accurately.

In the laboratory, Sara and her team got to work. FISH was the first step to investigate the chromosomal abnormalities for suspected Leukemia. Leukemia is a cancer of blood-forming tissues. The type of Leukemia depends on where it develops (lymphoid or myeloid cells) and the rate of growth of the cancer. Acute Leukemia appears suddenly and grows quickly, while Chronic Leukemia appears gradually and develops slowly over months to years. Based on both these criteria, there are four types of leukemia: Acute Lymphoblastic Leukemia (ALL), Chronic Lymphocytic Leukemia (CLL), Acute Myeloid Leukemia (AML), and Chronic Myeloid Leukemia (CML).

FISH was a preferred diagnostic tool for Leukemia since FISH could be used to check for an abnormality within the Philadelphia chromosome (Ph) often associated with Leukemia. This abnormality results from a reciprocal translocation, a genetic rearrangement, between chromosomes 9 and 22. In this translocation, a portion of chromosome 9 fuses with a portion of chromosome 22. The abnormality was named when researchers discovered it at the University of Pennsylvania in Philadelphia. Sara carefully smeared the sample onto the slide. She then put the slide through the FISH procedure and added fluorescent probes designed to target specific regions of the chromosomes. As she looked closely through the microscope, she saw the colored spots lighting up, indicating potential abnormalities in the sample's chromosomes. She detected an interesting pattern for this abnormality. There was one fusion of the ABL gene located on chromosome 9 to the BCR gene located on chromosome 22 and two normal ABL signals and two normal BCR signals.

FISH was helpful to confirm the presence of a Philadelphia chromosome abnormality. However, Sara needed more details to get a bigger picture and to detect other abnormalities. She decided to perform karyotyping, a technique to visualize all the chromosomes at once. The team cultured the cells from the blood sample, arrested them during cell division, and stained the chromosomes to create a karyotype. When the karyotype was ready, Sara analyzed it meticulously. Her trained eye spotted an anomaly—a piece of one chromosome had broken off and attached itself to another. This translocation was likely the root cause of the patient's condition. The karyotype result was interesting. She saw a rare abnormal condition where two normal chromosome 9's and two normal chromosome 22's with one extra chromosome masquerading as parts of chromosome 9q and chromosome 22q fused. As a result of this karyotyping, Sara suspected a subtle genetic variation might be contributing to the overall picture.

To probe deeper, Sara decided to use microarray technology. Microarrays would allow her to scan a patient's DNA for smaller variations, such as copy number changes and single nucleotide variations. Copy number changes refer to variations in the number of copies of a specific DNA segment or sequence within an organism's genome. These changes involve duplications, deletions, or other alterations of genetic material. Copy number changes can have significant implications for an individual's health. Single nucleotide variations (or SNV) are a type of genetic variation or mutation that involves a change in a single nucleotide (the building blocks of DNA) within a DNA sequence. Sara loaded the patient's DNA onto the microarray chip and initiated the scan. The sophisticated equipment quickly generated a comprehensive genetic profile. As the results appeared on the computer screen, Sara's heart raced. She identified several genes associated with developmental disorders having abnormal copy numbers in the sample DNA. It was becoming clear that the young boy had a complex genetic condition resulting from both the chromosomal translocation and smaller genetic variations.

With their findings in hand, Sara and Emily contacted Dr.Rodriguez at Emmanuel Hospital to deliver the news. Sara prayed beforehand over the case, and she prayed that Dr. Rodriguez would have the wisdom to create an appropriate plan for the young boy's treatment. Emily explained the diagnosis and the implications for the boy's treatment. Through the genetic analysis they were able to confirm the presence of Acute Lymphoblastic Leukemia (ALL). Together with the doctor, they formulated a comprehensive treatment plan addressing both the chromosomal translocation and genetic variations. Although Sara did not have a direct interaction with the patient, she was instrumental in developing the plan for the patient's treatment.

Days turned into weeks, and Dr. Rodriguez began the treatment for the patient. Sara's dedication to her work had given the boy a fighting chance. She knew that cytogenetics tools like FISH, karyotyping, and microarray are not just instruments in a lab; they were lifelines to patients providing answers, hope, and a path forward in the complex world of genetics. Testing of samples may be trivialized like a simple analysis; however, there are several people involved in making the analysis accurate and thorough to improve decision making plans and best patient care.

In the months that followed, Sara and her team continued to support the family by monitoring the young boy's progress and adjusting his treatment plan. After a few years of treatment, the boy's health gradually improved. Sara was happy to see her prayers answered. Sara was reminded once again of the profound impact Cytogenetics could have on the lives of patients and their loved ones. She remained committed to unravelling the genetic mysteries that came her way, one chromosome at a time, and making a difference in the world of medicine.

# GOD OF IMPOSSIBILITIES

## Novin John, MD

Becoming a doctor was a big dream, and finally, after finishing, I thought, "What next?" During my career, I was privileged to be a CMF (Christian Medical Fellowship) Kerala Group member. We met daily for hostel prayers, weekly on medical school campuses, quarterly for regional conferences, and yearly for the annual conference. My dream in medical school was to see highly accomplished, wealthy, and famous doctors and to be like one of them. During medical school and as part of the fellowship, we visited remote rural mission hospitals where I witnessed super-specialized doctors silently doing brilliant work without pomp or accolade. This intrigued me to shift my focus toward the real heroes. On our way back, I prayed on the train, "Lord, in Your will lead me towards missions."

After medical school, my sister encouraged me to take the USMLE to come to the USA. I borrowed a Kaplan study guidebook to prepare and started to read, but my heart was unsettled. I remembered those mission trips and experiences in my training days. I stopped reading then and spent time fasting, praying, and asking the Lord for His guidance. I received Psalms 138:8, and I received peace, knowing that the Lord would lead me. Around that time, my dear friend Dr. Steve was leaving for Bihar, and I thought of joining him for 2 months. This journey then extended for 2 years, enriched with experiences beyond words and brought peace in my heart. After completing my training in anesthesiology at the Christian Medical College at Vellore, I returned to the mission hospital, where I worked with my wife, Dr. Angel, and my son Nathaniel. Now, as I was a consultant, new challenges arose, and responsibility was elevated. With time, God expanded my role to serve as the Hospital's Medical Director.

One day, I was called to the ER, where a young man was brought in by the border security forces at the Indo-Nepal border. He was comatose, hypothermic, without a blood pressure or peripheral pulse reading. We began resuscitating in full swing with chest compressions and intubation as part of the protocol for an unconscious patient, and I shifted him to the ICU. The border officers said he came from Nepal and probably drugged and overdosed and fell into a small canal. In the ICU, he remained comatose. We started vasopressors (blood pressure elevating medicine) and placed warm blankets around him. We named him 'Anonymous' as we didn't know his identity. Over time, his vital signs and urine output improved, and by the third day, his GCS (Glasgow Coma Scale – a measure of consciousness) changed, and he started responding. A liver panel was ordered (routine lab work), showing he was hepatitis C positive, common among IV drug abusers. Since he was taking illicit drugs, the usual sedatives didn't work on him, and he needed more anesthetic-potent medicines to control him. Once he woke, we desperately desired to know who he was and where he came from.

Meanwhile, his oxygen levels dropped, and an X-ray showed bilateral shadows suggesting Covid 19. The COVID-19 pandemic was spreading rampantly around the world at that time. We wondered if he was COVID-19 positive. He remained Anonymous, and the hospital continued to bear the costs of his ventilation and ICU stay, costing lakhs (equivalent to thousands of dollars). The consultants and management discussed the feasibility of continuing treatment without clarity on what we were treating. Was it COVID-19? He was in the common ICU, and none of us wore PPE (Personal Protective Equipment). Neither did we have formal permission from the government to treat COVID-19, and such cases had to be referred to government-designated centers.

One afternoon, the junior resident monitoring the ICU approached for further plans on keeping or referring him outside. He was using valuable resources potentially more beneficial for another patient, his cost of stay was escalating, and there was no family to claim his identity. I had to prepare an answer for my superior. My mind was conflicted, so I quieted myself before God and His word. Here was a young man on an ICU bed, unknown, wrecked because of his addiction. I pitied him and asked the Lord for help. I faced the dilemma of discontinuing treatment here only to send him to some government facility, knowing he would die the same day or end route being an outcast. No one would touch him because of his HCV status and possible COVID-19 infection. God presented the scene of Abraham serving the strangers, reminding me of God's unconditional forgiveness despite our failings. Prayerfully, we decided to continue treating him. The nurses were willing to continue care despite his HCV and possible COVID-19 status. I thought he had ARDS (Acute Respiratory Distress Syndrome) from drowning. He needed advanced antibiotic regimens and maximum ventilator support. Our security staff actively pursued tracing his identity through various sources. They put his photo on Facebook, and within three days, his stepbrother came to the ICU and recognized him.

The next day, his mother walked into the ICU, and I sensed tremendous relief and assurance in my heart that I had made the right decision to treat him. The next day, his wife came weeping, not sure if he would make it. By the grace of God, through fervent prayers, sacrificial nursing care, and tirelessly working with junior residents, he improved, and we shifted him to a step-down unit. We counseled him and shared the good news about our loving savior, Jesus Christ, with him and his family throughout his recovery. Soon, he was discharged with 95% of the hospital costs written off and went home with his family. It was a homecoming for their lost son. We then shared the address with local pastors to follow up with his family.

His recovery was miraculous. God helped us make the right decision despite his clinical state. This is now one of many miracles I witnessed firsthand in my medical career through missions. In missions, we see God in action, using our minds and bodies to bring impossibilities to reality. As I write this, many patients come to mind where I witnessed God's healing on them from their death bed. I'm grateful to the beautiful, caring, selfless nursing staff, colleagues, chaplaincy, family, and management for helping me change this young anonymous man's life. All thanks, praise, and glory to our Lord and Savior Jesus Christ.

# EVEN IF

## Samuel John, MD

In faith, there is enough light for those who want to believe and enough shadows to blind those who don't. - Blaise Pascal

There are few words in the English language more pregnant than the word "if." Within the confines of these two letters holds the expanse of all options, all possibilities, all hope. My time caring for children and their families diagnosed with cancer has imparted to me the power and also the dread of "if."

I have seen it in the eyes of nearly every parent, and every child old enough to understand, from the first moment we use the word "cancer." It is a look that searches for something to grasp onto, something in the beyond to secure them, something to tell them they will make it safely to that place. We carefully walk through the treatment plan, side effects that would likely occur, toxicities we hope will not, summed up with our stated goal to cure - that this disease will go away and hopefully never return. We review prognosis but will often not speak in absolute percentages, as the one child sitting in front of me at that moment is the one who matters one hundred percent. But without fail, be it on day one in the calamity of a new diagnosis, or day seven as the mind slowly begins to process what has happened in the past week, the question will surely come: what if?

What if chemotherapy doesn't work? What if the nausea and vomiting are so bad, she can't eat? What if he picks up an infection and his body is too weak to fight it? What if this disease goes away, but it does come back? What if I die from cancer? At times, I can provide answers, ones that I hope will encourage, instill hope, but also laid with the truth that there are many unknowns. It is the infallible truth of medicine we all must confront; there is much we do not know.

There are seasons where I struggle being in this space. Isn't my job to fill this void with the answer of how to heal? But just as our patients and families have their what-ifs, I often ask my own version when the next treatment step is not clear, when there is no obvious right answer, when the right answer may be no answer. Sometimes cancer cannot be cured. As much as we fight for healing, pushing the body to the brink of what it can tolerate, there comes a moment when we realize what we are fighting for must change. The collective where we shift our efforts from prolonging the number of days to pursue value in the day itself. But how can anyone possibly do this when the days are for that of a child?

To this question, I did find an answer. It came written in bold white letters on the wrist of a teenager with multiple relapsed brain cancer. He and his family wore his orange cancer bracelet as they journeyed together one final time. I met Robby when I was a senior resident on the Pediatric Oncology service. He was a fan of baseball, always kind to his sisters, with a heart as big as his dad's. This is how his mother described him. Through countless rounds of chemotherapy, radiation, and surgery, he knew his latest relapse was different, everyone did. They decided as a family that they would fill his days being home together, not spent in the hospital trying more therapy that was far from likely to be effective against his disease. Family, friends, teammates, and teachers were constant company until the day Robby was no longer responsive at home.

We admitted him for end-of-life care. A tragic phrase in itself knowing death was not far off, but he and his family had to first walk through the pain of dying. We treated pain caused by the spread of his tumor, we alleviated air hunger when his drawn-out gasps broke the silence and stillness of the room, but the salve for the grief of loss was not one we had provided. As Robby breathed his last, his giant bear of a father held his daughters under one arm, his wife under the other, as they all huddled around their son, their brother, this final time on his hospital bed.

Standing beside them, listening for the absence of heart sounds, I nod to his nurse to confirm the time of death; I can still see the bold white words on their orange bracelets: Daniel 3:17-18. I reached for my Bible when I got home later that night, needing to know what these verses said. They came from the story of the three Hebrew boys thrown into the fiery furnace. As a child, as a family walking through cancer, I could understand the reason and even pray with fervor for verse 17 embossed in silicone, "If that *is the case,* our God whom we serve is able to deliver us from the burning fiery furnace, and He will deliver *us* from your hand, O king"- *NKJV*

But how do you choose to include verse 18? Even before the trajectory of the journey is known, even before the first, second, or third relapse, even before the prospect of death becomes a reality, how can you embrace verse 18? *"But if not, let it be known to you, O king, that we do not serve your gods, nor will we worship the gold image which you have set up."*- *NKJV* Their orange bracelets declare the story of an unrelenting conviction of who God is. Even if cancer takes my life, even if we bury our son, our brother, even if the story did not end the way we so desperately want it to, You are still God.

I have learned that I may not, and most times will not have the answers to all the what-ifs that arise as we journey through illness with a family. But more importantly, I have also learned how much we in medicine need this space, this void. I stand convinced this is where God, the Great Physician, the true Healer, Peace himself, operates. Sometimes He asks us simply, to not interfere.

While I can also recount stories of the miraculous in ways we are accustomed to listening for, verse 18 reminds me that faith is not founded solely on outcomes, nor does this truth yield to troubles. Our God is in the ifs, and He will remain God through the even ifs.

# OPEN EYES AND EARS TO HEAR

## Alin Joseph, MD

When the pager is buzzing, the notes are piling up, the patients are anxiously waiting, and your name is being called repeatedly, it feels like there are never enough hours in the day. A medical professional's attention is constantly being pulled in many directions. Over time, we build up a hyper-focus that allows us to complete each task directly in front of us. But does that focus cause us to miss opportunities to serve those around us?

One Sunday morning, I was on-call, covering consults at several hospitals around Massachusetts. As with most weekends on-call, a busy unrest flooded my mind. There were just too many things to do, and with each minute, more items were added to the unending to-do list.

While driving between hospitals with that overwhelmed feeling, I took a moment to pray. It's often the farthest thing from my mind on busy days like that, but in that moment, I was reminded of a God in perfect control, even in the chaos of my day. That prayer helped me take a breath and a detour toward the church.

On that specific Sunday, my husband was preaching at a different church location, one that we would not typically attend but one that was closer to the hospital. I decided to join my family there. He was speaking from the life of David and all that God was doing in the mundane and obscure moments of his life to prepare Him. I sat next to an older couple I did not know. Thankfully, God knew them.

When the service concluded, I grabbed my things to return to that day's stress. Before I could run to my waiting patients, a pastor at that church introduced me to the elderly couple I had been sitting next to. The gentleman had served the Lord as a professor of theology, an author, and a Biblical scholar for many decades. That morning, he woke up and prayed. He sensed the Holy Spirit prompting them to attend the specific campus of that church. Neither of us knew why at the time, but we sat side-by-side.

During our conversation, he and his lovely wife took turns sharing their recent health struggles and even other challenges they faced throughout their nearly 70 years together in ministry. I had patients and colleagues waiting, but I knew the Lord needed me to open my eyes and listen to them.

As he began telling me about his most recent health struggles, he let me know that he was being plagued by continuous weight loss and fatigue. He had seen numerous physicians and undergone various blood tests and imaging studies. Ultimately, a bone marrow biopsy revealed a new diagnosis of amyloidosis. Filled with uncertainty about the diagnosis, they came to church that morning bearing the burden of a troubling diagnosis combined with a treatment plan that simply wasn't working.

There is no way they could have known this. Still, throughout my training and years of practice, I had seen an uncanny number of amyloidosis cases and witnessed its destructive capabilities. It is a process causing fibrils to deposit in numerous areas, some in the nervous, cardiovascular, and even the kidneys. Because of the disproportionate number of renal amyloid cases I had seen, I was able to develop deep relationships with leading specialists who would be able to help treat and manage the specific disease process this gentleman had been facing. But I needed to see God at work through it all.

There is no way this was a simple coincidence:

- I would be working that weekend and be led to attend church.
- My husband would preach at a different church location that weekend, closer to the hospital where I worked.
- This couple would be directed in prayer to attend that same church.
- We would sit right next to each other.
- He would ask for prayer from a pastor who knew I was a physician and would introduce us to each other.
- He would be praying for direction in dealing with the very disease with which I had a unique history.

I had so much to do that day, but it became clear that God needed me to open my eyes and listen to His guidance. I quickly created a summary and connected him with one of my colleagues, a world-renowned oncologist who regularly treated patients with amyloidosis. With this introduction, he could be seen within 48 hours, and his course of treatment was adjusted. That seemingly random interaction helped this man of God regain so much of the health and strength he had lost. Now, four years later, God continues to use him for his glory.

Seeing God at work is often hard amid chaos. Every step, every decision, and every interaction can feel random and disconnected. However, when we've placed our trust in Christ, the Holy Spirit is at work *while* we work. Interactions and decisions are no longer random but part of a divine plan to use our gifts for God's glory. It all starts with open eyes and ears to hear.

# ANGELS IN THE MIST

## Prabhu L Joseph, MD

Prakash woke up in a foggy haze. He didn't know what had woken him up. Was it the noise of the train or the angry screaming lady sweeping the platform around him? He didn't know nor did he care, nor could he care. His entire life was a foggy mist of sounds, people, names, and memories. Memories so vague and disconnected he couldn't stitch them together anymore. The next thing he remembered was the shocking hunger pangs gnawing within his belly. He looked around and found a half-eaten bun. He chewed it noisily, not trying to remember who had given it to him, not that he could remember anyway. He got up and took a few steps before being knocked down by a huge moving object. A sharp almost sickening pain shot through his left leg like someone had bitten it off. Screaming in pain he was pulled away from the train by some onlookers.

It was about 4pm when I was summoned to the casualty to see a man with an injury to his leg. I saw a man in his twenties lying on the emergency table with a cloth caked in blood and dirt wrapped around an obviously mangled foot. The emergency staff told me the police brought him and left him in our emergency department: a common practice for the railway police having nowhere else to take unknown patients run over by trains. We got down to clean his foot and dressed it up. Mangled beyond repair, we decided to perform a below knee amputation. We asked to speak to his family or nearest kin and were told he had been living alone on the railway station platform. He was apparently `mad` and lived there for many years. We decided to proceed with the surgery and he was operated and kept in the surgical ward. We called our psychiatrist who diagnosed him with schizophrenia and began antipsychotic medications, gradually seeing slow recovery.

Days went by and Prakash found himself in a soft clean bed. The pain decreased but he didn't feel like the foot existed. He felt like his foot was floating and devoid of any sensation. Faces and sounds became clearer. He remembered his name, his memory got stronger and he could recollect his family. He felt hungry, sad and happy. Emotions made sense and he could connect his thoughts to them. Our staff spoke to him and he managed a few coherent sentences each time they spoke.

When asked for his identity and his birthplace, Prakash remembered the name of his village, his father and his brothers. He couldn't remember phone numbers or addresses but he knew his surname. He belonged to a Mahadalit community, three hundred fifty kilometers away from where he was found. We searched his village on Google maps and were overjoyed to see its location. We found the nearest police station and called the inspector who knew a connection who could help find his family.

We finally got the number from an elder at the village Panchayat (governing body), a few days before Christmas. The man, overjoyed, told us he knew the boy and his family. It was Christmas and Prakash would find his family. On Christmas Eve I spoke to his father, but it became obvious the family did not share our exuberance. I was asked about the hospital bill. I told them they need not pay or worry but please come and take him. Their next question threw me off. They asked me how much he had earned. He left over a decade ago and they didn't want him back without anything to show for it. He was a liability and a burden which suddenly became obvious. Young Prakash, with his schizophrenia, was a huge burden to a poor Mahadalit family. Their limited resources were drained, treating him, taking care of him, and protecting him till they finally gave up and let him go, never to search for him.

I was stunned. Suddenly the magic of Christmas was not to be. Instead, it would be dark where this family clearly did not want their member back. I struggled with the unexpected change in Prakash's reality. What would we do to him? Send him back to the platform with his lower limb stump? Did we do all this to send him back to the misery he came from?

We got together with our community team and decided to take him to his village. We fitted him with a prosthesis and stocked him up with 3 months of medicines so he would not run out. We took a team and educated the village on mental health and its consequences. It looked like the village understood and were willing to take care of him. We got back to a brighter Christmas season and over the next few weeks forgot about him. I frequently remembered him and wondered what happened to him. Coincidentally I met a doctor working with the government in the very same village we left Prakash. He promised to let me know his whereabouts. A month later this doctor called me to tell me Prakash ran away again. No one knew where he went or what happened to him. I hope Prakash is safe and finds his way back home. Mental health is a killer in India. With not enough psychiatrists and a nonexistent understanding of mental health, millions in India's rural hinterlands suffer, their families suffer in a foggy darkness without hope.

I hope God keeps Prakash safe with his angels. Prakash may have sunk back into the foggy mist of schizophrenia but God still cares for him. The need for psychiatrists in places where the mist of mental illness is thick and heavy is unprecedented. Till then we can only hope for angels in the mist.

# CAMBODIA 2022: GOD'S PROMISE FULFILLED

## Sophie Joseph, RN

The Cambodia medical camp mission was a blessed experience for our team and personally life-changing. Working alongside a strong, motivated, and kingdom-minded team was a delight. Over four days, 616 patients were seen in two outpatient clinics, one in the village and one in the city. We provided medical care and health education to communities living in abject poverty, where resources and quality health services were extremely limited or difficult to access. Our trip aimed to provide medical care to the poor and needy and to declare the gospel of Jesus Christ.

We read in Isaiah 14:24 (NKJV), *"The LORD of hosts has sworn, saying, "Surely, as I have thought, so it shall come to pass, And as I have purposed, so it shall stand"* My expectations were not necessarily all God had planned for this medical mission trip. To truly understand the depth of its impact, let me rewind 12 years. During my early college years, a guest speaker spoke one day on the topic of modern-day slavery. For the first time a heart-wrenching and horrifying topic impacting the world illuminated my mind. Human trafficking as the most common form of modern-day slavery and as the fastest-growing criminal enterprises globally emerged in my mind. With increased exposure to this topic, God placed a burden on my heart to seek opportunities to help rehabilitate these young, victimized survivors. In 2011, my grandmother and best friend spoke privately to me about how she had seen visions of me serving the Lord among young children in parts of Asia, including Cambodia. Soon after, during a Sunday service at my local church, I heard about David and Liney Chacko, founders of a nonprofit organization called Global Renewal. This couple began a ministry with a vision to rescue trafficked children in third-world countries to bring them to the saving knowledge of Christ. I decided to reach out to David and Liney Chacko through social media to share what God had been speaking for my life. We exchanged a few messages, and I left the conversation encouraged and hopeful that one day, God would open a door for me to work among rescued children. I did not know when this vision would come, but I trusted God would fulfill it in His perfect time. During the waiting period, I continually prayed for the freedom of the children affected, for justice and the repentance of the traffickers, and God to bring an end to human trafficking. As the years progressed, my desire to serve the Lord grew stronger.

Fast forward to 2022, when God's promise was fulfilled. On the first day of our medical mission camp in Cambodia, a few of our leaders arranged an informal evening meeting with some residential team members from Cambodia. After our daytime medical camp, we traveled to a local restaurant to eat dinner, and soon after, a familiar couple walked in: David and Liney Chacko. This was a divine moment. I was in shock but simultaneously overjoyed. Tears filled my eyes. I greeted Liney and asked if she remembered our conversation ten years ago. I hastily scrolled back through a decade of conversations and pulled up the message to help jog her memory. We embraced, and I began to weep. After a team meeting filled with conversation and prayer, we decided to spend our last day in Cambodia serving young, rescued children alongside the Global Renewal team. The young teenage Sophie, who desired to serve among rescued children, was now seeing her dream come to life. God's ways and thoughts are higher than human understanding, and I am so thankful God created an opportunity for my path to cross again with David and Liney.

On the final day of our trip, a few of us were allowed to provide routine care for over 35 rescued children from a safe house in Cambodia. It was touching and life-giving to listen to the miraculous rescue stories of healing on these precious young lives from unfathomable trauma, and to see the joy of the Lord in their eyes and through their smiles. They were some of the most loving little children, hugging and thanking us for providing medical care.

My favorite moment was worshiping Jesus together. Seeing the enthusiasm and their love for our Lord through loud praise with the experience of freedom, despite their hardships, brought conviction to my heart. What a testimony! These beautiful survivors were making their mark in the world, all for the glory of God. During our time there I was overwhelmed with joy and gratitude in the presence of God and even now, thinking about God's faithfulness. The way things fell into place and the timing of our trip to Cambodia was undoubtedly God ordained and has now increased my faith in the Lord. God truly fulfills the desires of our hearts in His time.

It was indeed an honor and a humbling experience to serve the people of Cambodia, to share the gospel and love of Jesus, and to pray with them. We could feel God at work from the beginning until the end. There is still so much work to be done. Our prayer for the nation of Cambodia is that the Gospel of Christ would transform the lives of individuals filling them with hope and love that only comes from above. I am grateful to God for a memorable and eye-opening experience during my medical mission trip. I pray that my testimony encourages others to step out and serve as the hands and feet of Jesus.

# MAKE A JOYFUL NOISE TO THE LORD

## Tony Joseph, MD

*Psalm 100:1–2, NKJV- "Make a joyful shout to the LORD, all you lands! Serve the LORD with gladness!"*

After working in the medical field for a few years, you start to see the routines of life. People become hardened in their ways and cynical of each other. Over time, the empathy we show to people decreases, and we become critical of their plight. During the recent pandemic, people showed more care; however, this was temporary. It is now uncommon to see those serving others doing it out of the joy in their hearts. However, seeing people displaying the joy of the Lord and helping others is unique and life-changing.

During the few mission trips I participated in, I experienced missionaries displaying this joy in serving their fellow man. They were not concerned with themselves but understood the needs of their fellow sister and brothers to help them. They visited people; although some villages were unsafe, they understood the risks of serving in those communities.

In 2009, I participated in the Navapur convention in North India. It was a week-long convention where thousands of people attended. Most were from the surrounding villages without proper health facilities and sparse medical care. Hearing of these conditions, the convention leader wanted to serve them. They collaborated and organized a medical camp with local doctors and healthcare providers during the convention. This gained a doctor's attention from rural Oklahoma, who eventually attended the convention and served the villagers.

The medical camp coincided with morning meetings where several hundred were seen daily. Local doctors saw nearly all the patients who had registered for the medical camp. Essential treatments including minor wound care, medications, and nutrition packs were given. One particular brother came to the camp with an open wound present for over a month, with wound healing needing debridement. Due to its size and lack of current resources at the clinic, the team could not take any dramatic steps.

The visiting doctor from rural Oklahoma saw this man's large wound. Because he had brought his equipment, he debrided the wound and applied salve over the wound area. The procedure hurt a bit but was lessened by the joy of a well-dressed wound. Even though the doctor could not communicate well due to language barriers, they connected, and their faces conveyed heartfelt gratitude and thankfulness. The doctor felt gratitude for this opportunity to care for this patient.

A few days later, the patient returned to see the doctor and, through a translator, spoke to him. The patient conveyed his thankfulness and brought his family members with him. Through a translator, we learned he wanted his family to participate in the convention and hear the messages from the servants of God. Hearing this news brought much gladness to the organizers. Being a helping hand to these people encouraged the medical team to do more. Over the years, a small clinic began, and now, yearly, a medical camp is being organized during the convention season.

As it says in Matthew 25:40, *NKJV* - "And the King will answer and say to them, 'Assuredly, I say to you, in as much as you did it to one of the least of these My brethren, you did it to Me.' The weight of those words struck me. God has given us the resources, education, and privileges to be in a place of influence. It is our choice and mind that we use these resources to serve Him. Our service to others is related to our love for God.

Recently, I visited Wayanad, a place in the northern district of Kerala, a place of farming with many tribal groups. There is a jungle in that region where wild elephants, tigers, and leopards roam and where a few people have been harmed or killed by these animals. These tribal groups have no written language. Most villages have elders as spiritual leaders and their local witch doctor. During this visit, I met a fellow man of God. He studied in an Episcopal seminary 20 years ago. His father and older brothers worked as pastors/counselors in the tribal villages in Wayanad and a de-addiction center. He visited and helped them in their ministry during his studies. Witnessing firsthand God transforming the alcoholics in the tribal groups by counseling, prayer, and without any medications changed his perspective. He decided to leave his family and stop pursuing the priesthood. Instead, he is involved in ministry and leads a church in the Wayanad district.

Initially, working among these wonderful people was difficult. There needed to be a proper road, electricity, or communication channel with them. They did not have a written form of language (however, it is now written using the Malayalam alphabet, with the Bible being translated into their language). They also believed in many gods and witchcraft. One instance was when an older witch doctor's grandson was affected by a skin condition that lasted for a few years. The grandfather had gone to many witch doctors without receiving healing.

During his early ministry, the Pastor would visit this witch doctor to build a relationship with him and others in the village. As they were speaking, he mentioned his grandson was sick. The grandfather mentioned all the gods he prayed to and people he met to get healing for his grandson. He was in a place of desperation and asked the man of God to pray. The pastor began to pray; however, the young boy did not receive healing immediately. The pastor challenged the grandfather to accept Jesus as Lord and leave his false gods and the practice of witchcraft. The grandfather made a bold decision and said, " Yes." A few weeks went by, and the boy received complete healing. This completely changed the grandfather's view of the pastor and his ministry. Over the next few years, the witch doctor came to the Lord, saving his entire family.

As a result of the village people receiving the Lord, infighting stopped between villagers, and poor relationships were mended. People began working together, and a complete transformation occurred in the village. A village custom was to give alcohol to little children from the age of 4, but due to education, this stopped. Children were given guidance about the school, with many now educated (even the grandson who was healed is now a prominent leader in the local church). The pastor helped the village get a road, electricity, and other necessities. The grandfather, a witch doctor and patriarch of the village, previously constructed an area for worshiping idols. He destroyed the idol statue after his transformed life as a child of God. Currently, a church building is standing in place of the idol.

Serving people truly brings gladness to one's life and demonstrates God's love. I witnessed both Navapur and Wayand people being transformed. Through treatments using medication, surgery, counseling, and prayer, these ministers are God's hands and feet. This pastor in Wayanad embodied God's purpose for us to serve. His demeanor and caring attitude, through his smile, conveyed God's love. Seeing this, I am encouraged to do more and I urge you to do the same.

# CALL UNTO ME AND I WILL ANSWER

## Shejoy Joshua, MD

During my training as a neurosurgeon, I was taught that a good knowledge of brain anatomy along with fine surgical skill and self-confidence is sufficient to perform any case successfully. Following my training, when I began practice, I strived to achieve these strengths. But even then, the outcome of certain cases was out of my control and completely contrary to what I expected. With the margin of error being minuscule in neurosurgery, the patients will have long lasting or permanent deficits even with minor issues during the surgery. This put a lot of stress, fear and anxiety in my heart. The famous French Practitioner Rene Leriche stated - *"Every surgeon carries within himself a small cemetery, where from time to time he goes to pray- a place of bitterness and regret, where he must look for an explanation for his failures."*

Then I understood the need of prayer and depending on the Holy Spirit's guidance and help before starting every case. This reduced my anxiety and gave me peace during surgery. It also made a great difference in the outcomes. I have felt His grace, each and every time I called onto Him. I clearly remember one such instance I would like to share here.

Seven years back and early in my career, I received a call around 11 pm, from the ED physician, informing me a 10-year-old male child had been brought to the ER with a history of a bus hitting him. This happened at 5 pm, following which he was taken to multiple hospitals, all of whom had given up on him, since his pupils were dilated and he had no neurological response to any stimuli.

On arriving at our hospital, he was hemodynamically stable, but his neurological state remained poor. A computerized tomography (CT) of the brain revealed diffuse cerebral edema(brain swelling) with early features of hypoxic brain damage. Considering his age, the options discussed with the family were: continuing medical management or considering surgical decompression with very poor prognosis. They chose the surgical option even though the chances of survival were grim.

I planned to do a large decompressive craniectomy, to create space for the injured brain to expand, which is the norm in such cases. However, while raising the bone flap off the superior sagittal sinus (a layer between skull and brain covering), during the surgery, I encountered torrential bleeding. This was the site of the fracture line that had probably already torn the sinus wall. By the time I managed to raise the flap, he had lost sufficient blood, for his hemoglobin to fall to 3 gm/dL and went into severe hypotension (low blood pressure). He did not respond to blood transfusion or vasopressors (medication to raise blood pressure). The anesthetist decided to close the wound and shift him to the ICU.

This is when I began to pray and the Holy Spirit reminded me of **Psalm 91:15, NKJV** - **"He shall call upon Me, and I will answer him; I will be with him in trouble; I will deliver him and honor him"**. I raised a cry in my heart to the Lord Jesus, to help me in this trouble. Immediately, I got courage, peace and divine wisdom to suture the sinus wall. I had never done this before, and I had never seen my predecessors do in the last 10 years since I joined neurosurgical residency. To do it without microscopic assistance, in the middle of the night, in an emergency setting is almost impossible. But I depended on Him, and was able to successfully suture the sinus tear and secure homeostasis (control of bleeding). I completed the surgery and transferred the young boy to the ICU. The anesthetist and everyone else in the team had no hope for him to survive.

But by God's grace he gradually improved. He later underwent cranioplasty (replacement of the bone flap) after three months. He rejoined school after six months and now has completed his 12th grade. To God be all the glory! He is true to His word: *"Call unto me and I will answer."*

# AS YOU DO TO THE LEAST

## Joseph Kuruvilla, DO

I was initially approached about Sara by her pulmonologist. She presented with shortness of breath, and her chest CTA showed dilated pulmonary arteries. He asked that I see her urgently. I will never forget my first encounter with Sara. The children's hospital where Sara was seen is a remarkable facility designed to capture children's imagination to help offset the fear and angst they experience at medical facilities. Sara, however, was very different from most children; she was altogether unimpressed, nor was there any fear to be seen in her eyes. Her voice was unwavering. I recall asking her to march in place or pace the hallways to assess her cardiovascular response to limited exertion. I was at first startled by her flat refusal, which then brought a smile to my face, followed by outright laughter. As I learned about her storied life, I began to understand why.

Sara was born in China. When she was found not to

be a "healthy" baby, she was abandoned as an infant by her biological parents. She was discovered wrapped in a blanket under a bridge, from where her life transitioned to an orphanage. During the first few years of life, she experienced frequent pneumonias with empyema requiring repeated hospitalizations. The medical management she experienced was uncharacteristic of practice in Western medicine. Still, given the frequent recurrence of empyema, a chest tube was placed and remained inside for nearly 2 years. She underwent multiple resections of the affected lung and eventually underwent removal of the left lower lung. Years later, the cause of her recurrent aspiration cases of pneumonia was found to be secondary to a tracheoesophageal fistula, an abnormal connection between the esophagus or feeding tube and the trachea or central airway. This was unbeknownst to her medical team, which, upon discovery, the tracheoesophageal fistula was surgically repaired. Not surprisingly, her recurrent cases of pneumonia ceased, and the chest tube she lived with for 2 years was finally removed. The delayed diagnosis, however, cost her dearly. She spent a great deal of those years back and forth from the hospital and endured multiple surgeries, eventually costing her the majority of her left lung. The psychological impact of having chronic recurrent pneumonia with purulent drainage for nearly 2 years, poor nutrition, isolation, and the rejection of her own family must have been crushing. She watched helplessly as families adopted other children, but Sara was overlooked. As years passed, she became among the older children at the orphanage, fully aware that with increasing age, so also fades the hope for adoption. During her short life, she endured a great deal of suffering all alone. Very little indeed impressed this resilient little girl, and the circumstances of her life had left her hardened.

As they entered retirement, despite having raised their children into adulthood, Mr. and Mrs. Williams had a heart to serve, and it was their dream to adopt a child. They traveled overseas from the United States to adopt a child from Sarah's orphanage. They adopted a young boy, one Sara cared for and considered her baby brother. During her visit to the orphanage, Mrs. Williams felt a small hand on the back of her foot while climbing a flight of stairs. She stopped abruptly to search where it came from and found Sara's eyes gazing back at her. That unlikely encounter would change the course of Sara's life. Mrs. Williams almost instantly knew that even though she came to China intending to adopt one child, she would be leaving with two. Perhaps some would attribute this meeting entirely to coincidence, but the words from Jeremiah 29:1, *NIV* - "For I know the plans I have for you, declares the Lord," convinces me otherwise. Sara finally found the acceptance she had never known before and could remain with the young boy she loved and had already considered her brother.

By the time Sara saw me, she had developed significant progressive dyspnea, having to stop to catch her breath when walking from the parking lot to the clinic. She developed pulmonary hypertension, and after a battery of tests, including cardiac catheterization, we confirmed she had constrictive pericarditis. Yet another and most significant complication of her chronic recurring pneumonia that had likely caused her recurrent pericarditis, scarring, and eventual stiffening of the pericardium. This scarring leads to the inability of the heart's ventricles to relax, causing heart failure related to the elevated pressures in all the heart's chambers. She had only modest improvement in her symptoms with medications, and a difficult decision was to be made between two high-risk and high-morbidity operations: heart/lung transplantation vs pericardiectomy. Given the poor outcomes of heart/lung transplantation at that time, we elected to proceed with pericardiectomy.

Her surgery was successful; however, her postoperative course and time spent in the ICU were prolonged for months. Her reserve was low as a result of her diastolic dysfunction (poor heart relaxation), lung disease, and poor nutrition. Sara refused to eat anything made from the hospital and adamantly declined NG or G tube feeds. The introduction of enteral tubes unlocked suppressed memories and PTSD from her time at the orphanage, which she refused to revive. Throughout her months in the ICU, her father and mother never left her side. They alternated 12-hour shifts so that Sara would never be left alone. While one remained with her at the bedside, the other went home to rest and cook because it was the only food Sara would eat. I remember walking into Sara's room one morning to examine her, and my eyes welled up with tears when I saw Mrs. Williams kneeling on both hands and knees, washing Sara's feet in a basin. I always knew this family embodied the mind of Christ, but I don't recall ever seeing it on display at that very moment. The gospel can be preached publicly to reach thousands or to a lesser audience in complete silence, both effective, but its power is revealed when we see it take human form.

Sara made a slow recovery, and when she left the hospital, there was a parade of hospital staff to applaud her triumphant exit. Over the next year, I had the unique privilege of watching the Williams family create a lifetime of beautiful memories with Sara, from providing valuable lessons, gardening, local trips, weddings, family events, and even a trip to Disney World courtesy of Make-a-Wish. I was Sara's physician directing her complex care, but I also knew my purpose stretched beyond just their medical needs; I needed to address their emotional and spiritual needs as well. This was something I implored God in my prayers and began to see it answered in a way I did not foresee. I witnessed a child experience healing of a different nature, once so stoic and distant, now always smiling and reflecting transcendent joy uncoupled from the state of her health. She had found acceptance in a family that truly loved her and met love personified in Christ Jesus through them. A more profound form of healing had taken place in this young child.

Not surprisingly, Sara again developed recurrent restrictive cardiac physiology and worsening pulmonary hypertension for which there is no cure. Heart and lung transplantation was not an option the family wanted to pursue, a decision I respected. She returned to the hospital, and her condition quickly deteriorated. I witnessed Sara die peacefully in her mother's arms.

Mr. and Mrs. Williams are the unsung heroes of epic proportions in Sara's life, who humbled me and taught me many lessons I will always carry. I am eternally grateful to them for their trust. One of the many things I learned is that I need not permanently cure the disease to see healing take place. Modern medicine could not reverse her constrictive pericarditis, pulmonary hypertension, diastolic heart failure, PTSD, and the pain of being an orphan. Sara's primary turning point was not when she met me but rather the decision from Mrs. Williams to love selflessly that ultimately opened the door to her heart for the Healer who heals eternally. I shared this passage at Sara's funeral that closely describes Mr. and Mrs. Willams' actions over those few years:

> *For I was hungry, and you gave me food,*
> *I was thirsty, and you gave me a drink,*
> *I was a stranger, and you welcomed me,*
> *I was naked, and you clothed me,*
> *I was sick, and you visited me,*
> *I was in prison, and you came to me*
> *Then the righteous will answer him, saying,*
> *"Lord, when did we see you hungry and feed you, or thirsty and gave you drink? And when did we see you a stranger and welcome you, or naked and clothe you? And when did we see you sick or in prison and visit you?*
> *And the King will answer them,*
> *"Truly I say to you, as you did it to one of the least of these, you did it to me."*
> *Matthew 25: 35-40 (ESV)*

# PURPOSE REVEALED

## Daya Manmadhan, RN

God's plans are always great. The process of His work's fulfillment can be painful and difficult. Remember, silence does not equate inactivity. Though we may not see, feel, or hear from God, He is still at work.

> *"The Lord of Heaven's Armies has spoken—*
> *who can change His plans? When His hand*
> *is raised, who can stop Him?"*
> *Isaiah 14:27 NLT*

It was like any other Sunday. I went to church with my family, and at the end of service, announcements for the week reminded me of upcoming events. One was a Belize mission trip. I never thought anything of it, as I had several preoccupations: a mom of three kids, a wife, a homemaker, and a full-time administrative nursing supervisor. After service, a trip organizer asked if I would be interested in going. Unsure, I told her I needed time to think. We left church and in our car my husband asked me, "Do you want to go?" I responded, "How can I go, leaving the kids and work?" My husband replied, "If you desire to go, we will make it work." My children listened in on the conversation, and surprisingly supported my interest and assured me I need not worry about them for the week I was gone. Going on a medical mission was always a dream. Leaping on this opportunity, I texted the organizer in my car. Before I knew it, the organizing meetings began and preparation for the mission trip was in full swing.

In May of 2023, we arrived in Belize. I was excited to serve using my medical knowledge and to serve as an ambassador for Christ. Every morning before the day's work began, our team had a short prayer, and I remembered to thank God for this opportunity. Yet I had no idea why God chose me to come here, so I pleaded with Him to use me in ways He desired. One day, during our lunch break, one of our team members walked in quickly. We were enjoying our meals in the other room, while the clinic was still attending to pediatric patients. She came in, inquiring if a psychologist or social worker was among us. I knew we didn't have any on our team. But in the moment of need, through a quick impulse and decision, I told the pastor and team, "I'll go talk to them." Granted, I am a nursing administrator without any specific qualifications of a psychologist or social worker, yet instinctively, I felt I had to help this patient.

When I walked into the clinic, I saw a 13-year-old girl sitting on a small wooden chair. She had black hair with her head bent down avoiding any eye contact. She looked depressed and withdrawn. She spoke Spanish, so I asked for an interpreter. I said "hello!" She responded by saying "hello" back to me. I asked her what brought her here today, and she explained she was experiencing intermittent headaches and came with her aunt to seek help. She looked despondent, so I began to small-talk to break the ice. She was wearing a necklace with a half-heart shape on it. I asked her, "Who has the other half?" She shied away saying her best friend had it. I asked her, "Why are you sad?" Hesitating, she didn't open up. I shared about my daughter, who was just about her age. She started looking intently at me as though trying to seek help. I told her, "You know, we are here for a medical mission from New York, but I was sent here just for you so we could talk and I have a friend you should meet." I told her this friend was in our midst, listening to all our conversations. She then opened up on her sadness and requested I not share her secret with anyone in her family, including her mom or aunt. Her parents were separated when she was nine. Her father lives in Guatemala, and her mother lives here with her friend. Both her parents don't care much for the family. She has a younger sister and is worried about her well-being. She is frequently absent in school due to her inability to focus and lack of interest. She loved her dad and wanted him back and wished her parents were together. She felt the burden for her younger sister and for her future. I told the little girl even though she didn't share this news with anyone, Jesus knew it all. Jesus knows what you are going through. I believe God sent me here to introduce her to Jesus, a friend she needed, whom she could always talk to. I told her, "It's just like picking up the phone and speaking to any of your friends." I explained to her, you may not always see this person, but you can hear his voice if you listen carefully. I confidently told her she could always talk to Jesus, her friend. While I was speaking, her eyes started filling up and tears began rolling down her cheeks. I told her Jesus even sees those tears and He is already doing the work for you and your family.

In that short time of connection, it was as though these moments emphasized my purpose for coming. As I shared, the young girl started to trust me. She mentioned, "I'm afraid you're going to leave after three or four days of your trip." I told the little girl, "Yes, I will leave, but the one who came with me is here with you to stay! And guess what? You can talk to Him just like our conversation." The little girl couldn't stop crying. She embraced me and said, "I can't believe this!" I asked her, "Would you like to keep the friend I introduced you to? She excitedly responded that yes, she would love to keep this friend! I asked her if we could pray together. I walked to our pastor, who asked the local pastor to join, and together we prayed. The joy on this little girl's face was beyond description. She accepted Jesus as her personal savior, and I saw her sad face transform into a smile. Soon after we left Belize collecting our memories and experiences with us. However, this girl remained with the Lord and she continues to attend the local church and is serving the Lord. I can't wait to hear how she matures in her life with Jesus, the friend she met that day.

# A FAITH BEYOND
# HUMAN EXPERTISE

## Benson Matthew, MD

Understanding the human body's complexity was intriguing as I transitioned from high school to college and growing up in a spiritual Christian background was instrumental in appreciating God's masterpiece: His creation. It has been 14 years now, where 7 years were in active clinical practice. I have encountered countless patients with diverse illnesses and various backgrounds. Often our organs' vital functions are taken for granted until they malfunction and patients seek medical attention when their systems fail. God created and designed every organ in the human body with its own purpose. The Word tells us God created man perfectly; however, when he disobeyed God, sin entered the world, initiating the death process. We eventually face death. Disease becomes inevitable due to genetic, bodily, environmental, and lifestyle factors. However not every illness or disease leads to death. The Bible tells us of divine interventions and healings in many people. Thanks to modern medical advancements, countless diseases can be cured through medical and surgical interventions.

Nonetheless, death remains inevitable and is our final limit. When human efforts fail, comfort is the next objective, easing the pain of death in their final moments. I am humbled God has given me this opportunity to provide relief to people during these pivotal moments. My goal is to practice medicine and to elucidate the greater meaning of life and death. Jesus Christ is the only one who has conquered death. Only faith in Him can grant us eternal life. Being an ambassador for this cause is my mission and should be the mission of every believer. While God can give physical healings, the bigger picture shows us those who have received miraculous healings from God have ultimately succumbed to death. Death is our ultimate enemy, and its root cause is sin; where the Bible clearly states, 'the wages of sin is death.' Therefore, physical healings only serve as signposts leading someone towards the true God.

There seems to be a conflict between faith and medicine. The Bible states that prayer with faith in God can heal a person, from bodily sickness and also from spiritual sickness. In 1 Timothy 5:23, *NKJV* Paul advises Timothy, *"No longer drink only water, but use a little wine for your stomach's sake and your frequent infirmities."* Here we see the apostle Paul, whom God used to bring divine healing to many, advising his young disciple to use a human remedy to relieve him from a bodily symptom. From this, we understand that striving for a healthy life and striving to treat diseases should be our objective. However, despite significant medical advancements, preventing death is impossible. Diseases still lack a cure, many with only temporary treatments to control the symptoms.

Over the years, I've realized patients need more than medicine or human intervention; they need a spiritual encounter for a holistic approach. God has raised opportunities for me to pray for some of my patients in moments of deep need and compassion. Although I haven't witnessed miraculous physical healings, I have explained the spiritual implications of disease to connect God to my patients. Their responses are varied. When my patients have faith in God, I have witnessed spiritual healing occurring in their lives. Most times, not just illness causes distress, but also approaches to it. As a physician, seeing patients in distress is routine for me, allowing me a moment to connect the absolute truth to them. Jesus said, 'I am the way, the truth, and the life. We find life in Him.' As children of God, everything we do originates from Jesus. Without Him, we can do nothing.

# EXPERIENCING CHRIST

## Sini Paulose, DO

An old Malayalam song goes, "Nin dhanam njan anubhavichu, nin sneham njan ruchiarinju" and translates to "I have experienced your goodness, and I have tasted your love." This is one of my favorite Malayalam songs, and I often sing it with joy as I reflect on God's goodness and the love I have experienced throughout my life.

I came to this country as a teenager, and though I was transplanted at the age of fourteen, I had confidence that God was my refuge and strength and was ever present to help me in times of trouble (Psalms 46). I still remember the time I fell ill as a young child. A pastor prayed for me, and felt God had a plan for me to be in the mission field. God made a path for me to go to medical school and enter into family medicine, knowing God had a specific purpose for my life.

Throughout my career, I heard many stories of God working in people's lives. I witnessed the transforming power of God in so many lives. During my 3rd year of medical school, I went with a team of students and professors from CMDA (Christian Medical and Dental

Society) to Juarez, Mexico. We had a wonderful time worshiping God and meditating on his word together. Witnessing the dedication and passion they had for God was a transforming experience. We delivered much-needed care and resources to the needy community and received love and care from the beautiful people of Mexico.

From 2008 to 2015, I worked in refugee health in Lynn, MA. During that time, I met with some wonderful Bhutanese refugees from Nepal (living in impoverished conditions and refugee camps) and later came to the US through the UNHCR program. I met many Christians, and I still remember a Christian pastor named Mani working relentlessly for the Gospel. I was so impressed by these people loving God despite their circumstances.

In 2014, I spent a week on Tribal Missions in Attapadi, India, with Dr Muralidar. There, I saw how the love of God could transform lives and how the Gospel can impact entire regions through the vision of a few dedicated to God's work. Among them were Dr Muralidar, Dr Aleyamma, and many other physicians who dedicated their retirement lives to serving God. They lived in modest quarters while delivering much-needed health care to the tribal community of Attapadi and the surrounding areas.

In 2018, I teamed up with GHO (Global Health Outreach), a mission branch of CMDA, to go to El Salvador. It was my first experience of this kind since Mexico. Physicians and other health care practitioners from all fields of medicine, walks of life, and different regions of the US came together with one mission – to serve the needy of El Salvador for God's glory. I was privileged to work with people who genuinely experienced God's goodness, showing eagerness and passion to demonstrate God's love to others. We encouraged each other and testified to God's goodness in our lives. I heard many testimonies of God working in different people's lives in unique and unforgettable ways, bringing them closer to their Savior.

While in El Salvador, I learned there was a predominance of gang violence, and countless young people were victims of gang violence. Many joined them out of fear that they or their loved ones would be killed or assaulted. I encountered a grandmother bringing her young grandchild she took care of who was sick and dehydrated. The grandmother was distraught, sad, and filled with the burden of taking care of the young child while feeling the pain of her daughter being imprisoned because of gang violence. Hesitant initially, I prayed, and miraculously, we intervened at the right time to administer the proper treatment while sharing the Gospel with this grandmother. I knew it was the presence of God's hand at that critical moment.

God was operating miracles through other team members as well. The optometry team was busy providing much-needed eye care to the people whose vision was damaged by heat, smoke from fires (they burnt their trash outside the houses), and biogas used as fuel for cooking. The optometrist tried different lenses for one man with poor vision, and none of them would work. The team prayed, and suddenly, his vision was corrected with one of the eyeglasses they tried before. Many needed eye surgeries, and we sent them away. However, on the last day of our trip, the pastor heard from a group of ophthalmologists from South Korea planning to come to El Salvador and conduct eye surgeries - what a miracle!

In 2022, I connected with our local church in Lynnfield, MA, and partnered with Assemblies of God World mission to build a church and a well in the Masaai Mara region of Kenya. I went with the team to jumpstart the clinic. I witnessed firsthand the work of men and women to expand the kingdom of God in various ways – including providing care to the thousands of people living in the Kibera Slums (the largest slum in Africa) and the Masaai Mara region of Kenya. I saw the mighty hand of God moving as people came together to pray and provide medical care to the sick and needy. Later that week, I attended the church service with the Maasai people (tribal people inhabiting that land). It was a joy to witness them worshiping their Savior on mud floors without electricity, singing and praising God in their language. Their lives were transformed because missionaries went there and shared the good news of the Gospel.

Over the years of my medical career, I have witnessed God's transforming power in people's lives. On one such occasion, a woman in my practice suffering from alcoholism was delivered from it because God intervened in her life.

Another patient tells the story of nearly dying but receiving healing and coming back to life after having seen the light of heaven. I have experienced God's goodness in my life from my early childhood and continue to experience it. God delivered my children from the pangs of death – while they were in my womb. I started preterm labor at 20 weeks of gestation, but God preserved my twin boys in my womb till 33 weeks of gestation. They were born without any complications and they came home with us after spending only a few weeks in the NICU. God's love is real!

This has been an underlying theme of my life and my Christian walk. His hand of protection on our lives is real – all we need is to trust and turn our lives over to him.

# HOLDING ON TO
# PRAYER BEADS

## Shawn Philip, DO

My journey into gastroenterology began during the second year of my internal medicine residency. I was drawn to the vast array of pathology in the gastrointestinal tract and especially the variety of procedures where I could be hands-on and play a direct role in treating someone. We could perform colonoscopies for colon cancer screening and potentially prevent cancer. However, I did not know how many oncological cases I would handle until I started my fellowship. I had always heard of colon and pancreatic cancer throughout my training and its associated poor prognosis, but I never got first-hand exposure until my fellowship training. Cancer is a bewildering term to use in medicine and in Christianity. Its introduction to a room or conversation can shake a person's whole world and perception of life. It can make the strongest person in the world feel like a chaff in the wind and has changed families forever. The question of

" why do bad things happen to good people?" is always raised when discussing cancer. When my youngest uncle was diagnosed with multiple myeloma many years prior, I struggled with this question. Why would God choose to afflict someone with young kids and my family with such a diagnosis, which ultimately led to his demise? Little did I realize that it was this diagnosis that led to my family becoming closer to God. They began and still have weekly family prayers among themselves, which initially began to pray for my uncle. This has drawn them closer to God and further strengthened our relationship. How God can use these diagnoses to change the lives of people and those around them is astounding.

I was in my second year of a gastroenterology fellowship when I met Joe on his admission to the hospital. Joe was fifty-three years old and had lived a very fulfilling life. He was doing well until June, when he felt some mild abdominal pain. He got a routine CT scan, which revealed a pancreatic head mass. He eventually underwent an endoscopic ultrasound with a fine needle biopsy of the mass showing it was pancreatic adenocarcinoma (a type of pancreatic cancer). An oncologist was seeing him as an outpatient, but no treatment plan had been composed yet. He presented to the hospital two months later when I saw him due to pancreatitis that was felt secondary to his mass pushing on his pancreatic duct. I placed him on IV fluid hydration, and he began to improve with fluids and pain control.

On his third day of admission, it was less busy rounding that weekend; a weekend I was not supposed to work. My census was lower than usual, so I had time to make rounds with patients. I walked into his room and saw him with prayer beads in his hands. He called these beads his Misbaha. He had closed his eyes before I walked in, and I knew he was praying. He saw me, and seeing an empty chair next to him, I sat down feeling drawn by the Holy Spirit to connect with him. I asked him if he was praying. He told me that he was Muslim, that he would go once a month to the mosque but was not very religious. He told me he was praying because he had nothing else to hold on to. He was praying for hope and some peace. He told me his diagnosis of pancreatic cancer shook him to his core. He was very active and played soccer avidly for his whole life. He was very fit and told me he also drove a motorcycle every weekend. Joe showed me a picture of him on his motorcycle with his brother, which was his phone wallpaper. He had two older boys and one girl in high school. He was always healthy, so he kept repeating he had no idea how he could get such a diagnosis. He always thought nothing could bring him down in this world. He loved cars and told me about how he shipped a sports car recently to his country to have custom work done on it, and was awaiting its shipment back. He wondered if he would ever get to drive it. His daughter was just finishing high school, and wondered if he would ever see her get married and be able to walk her down the aisle.

I listened to his concerns and questions about his diagnosis. I answered him as best as I could that morning. We began to speak about religion after I commented on his prayer beads, as he said all religions are the same and that we have the same God. I knew that I had to speak about Jesus with Him. He was feeling empty and hopeless. I told him I know his religion stated Jesus was a prophet, but as Christians, we believe Jesus is the

Messiah and part of the Godhead. We believe He died for us to rid us of our sins, and we have a reason to live because of Him. He said he knew Jesus was important but did not know how much. I told Him about how even Jesus went through suffering. I shared with him the words of Jesus in Luke 22:42, *NIV- "Father, if you are willing, take this cup from me; yet not my will, but yours be done."* I told Him that even Jesus felt emotional turmoil before He gave His life, but He knew He had to go through it for us and that God had a plan for Him. My heart ached for Joe, and I did not know if I would see him again after today. I asked him if I could pray with Him. A nurse and another patient were in the other room, but I knew I had to lay my hands upon him and pray.

I prayed for Joe- for strength, healing, and for Jesus to touch and guide him throughout this difficult season in His life. I prayed for the Holy Spirit to speak to his heart and mind. He hugged me after the prayer. He did not expect a doctor to spend this long with him, especially sitting down to pray. We talked more about his family and his questions were geared toward whether he had a good prognosis or if he had much time. I knew I did not have those answers for him, but I told him I knew God had a plan and a purpose for him. It did not make sense now, but it would eventually.

I could see that Joe felt a sense of peace after I prayed with Him. My experience with Joe has led me to pray with other patients more. I know it has helped my spiritual journey. We may deal with many who identify with monotheistic religions like Islam and Judaism. Still, we must realize they may not know the importance of His sacrifice. It is tough to bring up these conversations with hospitalized patients as they are often in an acute disease state. However, when patients are dealing with diagnoses impacting them physically and emotionally, what could they lose from prayer? They have only the greatest gift to gain and a peace that can only come with prayer and fellowship.

Death is an inevitable route we all eventually will take. In the hospital, we see death so often it hardens our hearts. We become numb to its effects and think about it almost as routine. I have signed a death certificate and quickly move on to treat the next patient without a second thought. Our busy schedules make it almost impossible to connect with our patients and assess their spiritual needs beyond their healthcare goals. Sitting with a patient at the bedside, for even 10 minutes of your day, may be the most crucial conversation they will have. What if we could help their physical beings and their soul? Praying with your patients will help you treat them better and provide them comfort that many other sources cannot. I continue to pray for Joe and for Jesus to meet him wherever he is. Let us pray for the Holy Spirit to guide our minds and hearts as disciples to use prayer as a weapon for healing and to bring peace among our patient population. Let us pray God would provide us with the right situations and timings to facilitate a spiritual connection in or outside the hospital.

# A DIVINE APPOINTMENT FOR ETERNITY

## James Samuel, MD

*"Jesus went up on a mountainside and called
to him those he wanted, and they came to him.
He **appointed** twelve that they might be with
him and that he might send them out to preach
and to have authority to drive out demons."
"Who are my mother and my brothers?"
he asked...w**hoever does God's will** is
my brother and sister and mother."*
Mark 3:13-15, 33, 35, *Majority Standard Bible*

**M**ost of us who practice in an outpatient clinical setting are familiar with appointments. The appointments are generally given by the medical office to our patients. Patients are expected to come for their appointments on time and prepared with all the necessary medical information to help diagnose their problems. The patients expect respect, empathy to understand and help to sort out the problems they are facing. Often we go through these appointments as another chore in our daily professional routine. These appointments can be frustrating given the brevity of time we have with each patient to accomplish knowing the patient well, coming up with their diagnosis and treatment plan, and documenting the encounter with detail and accuracy. In the fast pace of our profession, we face high demands to provide satisfactory care to our patients, and at times lose sight of the fact that we are the ambassadors of Christ in this world. Every appointment with our patients is orchestrated by our Lord for us to be a representative of Him. That insight into our calling gives us the perspective of seeing each patient encounter as divinely ordained.

In one such divinely ordained appointment, I met a family of 3, a husband, wife, and a four-year-old son, referred to me by a good friend, an oncologist. The wife, thirty-one years old, was recently diagnosed with IgA nephropathy with nephrotic syndrome. She had made the appointment to establish care with me as her primary care physician. The family had just come from India a few months back, as the wife, a nurse by profession, was recruited by the local hospital here. She was the breadwinner of the house, but with the newly diagnosed nephrotic syndrome, she was unable to go back to work. The husband was unable to work as he was still updating his credentials and searching for a job. The disease had gripped the family with fear while they were navigating their life in a new country. She was started on prednisone, intravenous immunoglobulin, and cyclophosphamide; strong medications to treat the acute kidney failure. Her nephrologist started the conversation of potential dialysis if the treatment did not stabilize the kidney function. There was a sense of desperation in the room. I was six months out of my internal medicine residency working as a junior doctor in a multi-specialty practice. This case challenged me not only from a medical standpoint but as a social nightmare as the family had very little support. There in that room, I felt a compelling burden to help and a simultaneous feeling of helplessness engulfing me. I realized that only a divine intervention could bring healing to this family both physically and psychosocially. While taking her history I was led by the spirit to ask what Christian denomination they belonged to. I guessed they had a Christian background but I was not sure if they were saved. The husband answered that they belonged to a Jacobite background. He asked me what Christian background I belonged to and I answered I belonged to a Pentecostal background. The husband would later testify that when he first heard I belonged to a Pentecostal background, he detested me.

The visit included a quick focused physical exam. The exam confirmed significant swelling throughout the body due to protein loss from the kidneys. I concluded the visit by reassuring her I was available for her to reach out and willing to help in any way to facilitate the treatment process.

A few days later, the husband called and left a message through the contact center with a question regarding the medication. I called the husband back and while conversing, the Spirit of God led me to ask if I could come over to their home to pray with them. The husband welcomed my visit to their home. I called my uncle (my spiritual mentor) and another friend to come along for this patient's house visit. I never did a patient house visit before, and I knew medical care used to be practiced this way. But it was not merely a medical visit but a visit hoping we could share how God will come through for us when we trust him. They were welcoming, receiving us with great anticipation of comfort and strength. During that visit, we listened to their plight and we spoke about the gospel, that Jesus came into this world to bind our wounds and heal our souls, and that eternity with Christ is real and secure through an established relationship with Him. They were both open and willing to hear the word and we left the house thanking God for the opportunity to witness. They were relieved to receive the hand of support in a time of need.

In subsequent weeks, we invited them to come to our church. We began weekly contact with them either by phone or by visiting their home, providing them with much-needed fellowship and teachings from the Word. They received the Lord into their heart and eventually understood the importance of believers' baptism. They expressed their interest in obeying the will of God through public display of their newfound faith. On one Sunday morning, the husband and wife testified before the church how the gospel had changed them and nothing in this world, sickness or death would separate them from the love of God that is in Christ Jesus. With profound gratitude to the Heavenly Father, I witnessed the first baptism of a couple whom I met in my clinic. I was in tears, joyful to see the hand of God in all this and to see the family accepting Christ as their Savior and being baptized. This experience confirmed my calling that I was in the right profession practicing medicine and in the right place, according to the perfect will of God.

The family eventually became a catalyst in starting a new Sunday fellowship in our area with a renewed vision to reach out to the lost. They also started a weekly Bible study and prayer meeting at their home. The weekly meeting became a focal point for many other nonbelievers to come, attend and hear the gospel. Over the years they grew and matured in the Word and in the Lord's work. God used them to minister to their family members who also got the privilege to accept the Lord and get baptized. The family has been instrumental in teaching the word and leading various small groups and bible studies. God has blessed them in many ways and their testimony of God's grace, power and faithfulness has become a blessing to the church and others. It is a great joy to see how a single encounter in the clinical setting, inspired and led by the Spirit, has led to the salvation of many families and even provided the impetus for the creation of a church. I sincerely hope and pray that we are sensitive to the leading of the Holy Spirit in our clinical settings as we perceive every encounter and touch points as divinely appointed by God for us to be His witnesses.

# BE STILL

## Jemi Samuel, MD

It was Memorial Day 2015; I had been a hospitalist for seven years at the hospital where I completed my residency. I received a message asking for everyone's attendance at an urgent team meeting the next day. I instantly had an uneasy feeling. The next day, our hospitalist service director announced his resignation at the meeting with little to no transition plan. He was departing in a month and our team was summoned by the CEO. Since there was no one with much leadership experience it was announced that the hospital administration was going to explore management companies. Meanwhile six hospitalists were chosen to be part of the interim leadership team.

Unexpected breakdown of leadership and an unclear plan led to many others in the team choosing other opportunities, leaving us with less than half of the team. We soon realized that six people could not lead a team and a single leader was required to effectively manage the transition. I, being the senior most member, volunteered to hold the interim director position. In my mind it would be six months at the most and I would hand responsibilities over to whichever company was chosen then. Dr A, one of our nocturnists, volunteered to support me. Little did I know what I was stepping into.

The several months that followed were filled working as a full-time clinical hospitalist, hiring and managing an enormous number of locum providers to fill staffing challenges and participating in transition discussions with a big hospitalist management company the hospital had picked. Each day was long and stressful between managing the hospital workload and a family of three children with the youngest being a toddler. Dr B, my new boss, led the weekly discussions between the hospital and the company. The financial equation the company presented was too big for the hospital to afford. The agreement was revised several times and six months into this chaos, there was no resolution. By then Dr A and I became familiar with the ins and outs of leading a hospitalist group. We did not quite like the management company's approach towards our team.

In December 2015, Dr A and I halfheartedly decided to run the program on our own. We spent countless hours writing up a proforma though barely knowing what it even meant. Dr M, my mentor, helped formulate our thoughts into a business plan. Once we completed, Dr A and I approached Dr B with our proposal. Dr B listened to our ideas and startlingly dismissed us as amateurs and informed us proceeding with the management company was the right decision. We were confused and unconvinced it was the right path for us. Uncharted waters were before us and I was nervous about the huge task ahead of me. Perhaps this was God telling me I shouldn't do it.

I spoke to several family and friends the next few days

seeking counsel. Dr M reassured me I was capable of doing this and gave me her full support. So did Dr A. These people steered me to the verse, Esther 4:14, *NKJV* - *"Yet who knows whether you have come to the kingdom for such a time as this?"* I had three choices in front of me: watch my team disintegrate under a new regime, find a new job, or take the lead. The first two options did not seem right. I decided to persevere against the initial set back except I did not know how. I prayed for direction and counsel, repeatedly singing the song "Trust in you" by Lauren Daigle. Psalms 46:10, *NKJV* - *"Be still and know that I am God"* became my daily source of strength.

I did not know anyone in hospital administration. Dr B was my only conduit to leadership and an earlier attempt had utterly failed. I somehow needed to let the administration know my plans. Dr M mentioned to the hospital CEO that I had some ideas about hospitalist management. Days went by and the CEO did not reach out to me. I prayed that somehow God would grant me an entrance as he did for Queen Esther.

One day when I was walking into the hospital lobby I found myself in front of the CEO. He greeted me, though we never talked before, and asked me to schedule an appointment to meet with him. I was beyond thrilled but very nervous. Dr A and I approached the CEO's admin to schedule an appointment with much difficulty. Eventually we got onto his calendar at the end of January 2016. Dr A and I printed our slides and walked into the CEO's office. He was kind, listening to us and patiently taught us how to read department P&L (profit and loss statements). We thought we convinced him. Concluding the meeting, he asked me if I watched Shark Tank before. I said no. He then asked me to watch it and convince all the sharks. I walked out confused. Once I watched the show Shark Tank, I understood the battle was not yet over. We had not mentioned anything to Dr B who had been reporting directly to the CEO since the Chief Medical officer (CMO) resigned. I thought I would be fired the day Dr B found out what I had done. But I was at peace knowing I was in God's perfect will. It so happened Dr B had to go out on a medical leave.

Dr A and I met with every single person in senior leadership over the next few days presenting our plans. A new CMO was chosen by February, fully supportive of Dr A and I taking over hospitalist leadership. Despite the individual support from all members of senior leadership, the CEO was not ready to make a decision. Meanwhile I was interviewing candidates for all the open hospitalist positions and six new graduates agreed to join my team amidst the uncertainty.

On March 23, 2016 (Day of Purim) there was a senior leadership meeting to discuss the future of the hospitalist team. I was convinced this was going to be the day of deliverance. Dr B was presenting on behalf of the management company to convince the leadership. I requested permission to attend the meeting to speak for myself but it was denied. Dr A and I sat outside the conference room for 2 hours while our fate was being determined. The CEO walked out telling us he needed one more week to make up his mind.

The following week seemed like eternity. On April 1, 2016 I was sitting in my office when Dr B walked into my office. I was terrified. He uttered two words, "You won". I don't remember much of what happened afterwards. Dr

B asked me to proofread the announcement he wrote up, which I did. After he left my office, I ran out to the call room where Dr A was sleeping after working the night before. I knocked on the door like an impatient toddler. I delivered the good news to Dr A. We were both surprised, as it felt surreal. We went back to our office informing our small team who faithfully stood beside us despite all the challenges. Within the next few hours, Dr B sent out the announcement to all hospital staff appointing myself and Dr A as the director and associate director of hospitalist service, just the way Haman had to lift Mordecai up.

Within the next few months, we were fully staffed, stabilized and had no more temporary providers. I was moved to report directly to the CMO. Dr B went on a continuous medical leave until his departure in September. Seven years later, proud of the team I could build and lead, I can say with all of my heart, "My Lord Jesus is faithful and unchanging". If I knew what lay ahead of me, I would not have chosen this path in 2015. I am glad that His ways and thoughts are higher than mine.

Looking at Psalms 46:10 written on my office wall I wonder how marvelously God orchestrates everything including naming my firstborn, Esther 18 years ago! I expectantly wait for His next move in my life.

# COMFORT ALWAYS

## Jesintha Stevenson, MD

One of the greatest lessons I have learned in medicine was at the bedside of a dying patient in the ICU in my first year of residency. I went into medicine with quixotic hopes and dreams of solving complex puzzles and desiring to save lives in the nick of time. The ICU rotation was a busy month that held plenty of opportunities to participate in just that. Witnessing active dying was not part of this dream or desire, but this encounter taught me caring for patients means primarily to comfort them.

Our dying patient was a middle-aged man with advanced throat cancer. He had undergone many different treatments to control the cancer. They had worked for some time, but the cancer had progressed far, now blocking off his airway. He was placed on a ventilator for some time, but given his lack of improvement over several weeks, it was decided to take him off the ventilator and allow him to pass away. His family was distraught to watch him die, so his ENT surgeon decided to be present in his final moments while his family waited outside.

I was preparing to leave for home when my co-intern asked me if I wanted to be present to watch. I honestly didn't. I was at the end of my ICU shift and ready to go home to return next morning and learn further about the comparatively more exciting business of saving lives. At this point there was nothing else to be done to save this man's life. What could I possibly learn being present, and how could I hope to benefit this man, who was unconscious by then? But I felt an inner urge to wait. I am glad I did.

We stood silently and watched as the man's breathing tube was removed, and his oxygen levels started falling. Removing the tube caused bleeding from the tumor now pooling and filling up his airway. The oxygen levels continued to dip, too low to sustain life, and I had to will myself to stand still. My short time in the ICU taught me those oxygen levels typically required immediate and aggressive resuscitation. Doing nothing in the ICU, where the norm was a focused rush of activity to save lives and in this case improve oxygenation, seemed so wrong.

However, the ENT surgeon, exhausted from a long day full of rewarding surgeries and heroic saves, wasn't 'stationary.' I watched as he gently mopped the blood oozing from the tumor. He didn't have to. There were plenty of absorbent pads underneath that would have prevented a mess, and the patient was, by then, probably unconscious to feel blood. As minutes turned to an hour, I watched the surgeon patiently stand by holding the man's hand, not even checking his watch once. He could have gone home as he deserved rest; no one would have blamed him. But, in those seemingly meaningless moments, he nobly chose to comfort this dying man; to give him dignity. When the patient passed away, the surgeon proceeded to the waiting room to comfort the heartbroken family.

In that encounter, that ENT surgeon taught me the greatest lesson I learned in 'doctoring', and it was a simple one: 'cure sometimes, treat often, comfort always.' I had memorized the aphorism often attributed to Hippocrates and zealously desired to follow the first two directives but had often ignored the last. Yet isn't this what Jesus, the Great Physician, came to do? In Luke 4:18, *NKJV* Jesus quotes the prophet Isaiah who writes *'The Spirit of the LORD is upon Me, because He has anointed Me to preach the gospel to the poor; He has sent Me to heal the brokenhearted, to proclaim liberty to the captives and recovery of sight to the blind, to set at liberty those who are oppressed.'* And He calls us to do the same. *'Blessed be the God and Father of our Lord Jesus Christ, the Father of mercies and God of all comfort, who comforts us in all our tribulation, that we may be able to comfort those who are in any trouble, with the comfort with which we ourselves are comforted by God.'* (2 Corinthians 1:3-4, NKJV). In the busyness of examining and history-taking, treating and curing, documenting and billing, our primary duty is to strive and reflect God's healing comfort to everyone in our care.

# CAN WE JUST PAUSE…

## Blessy Sucharitha, MD

*"He who has pity on the poor lends to the LORD, And He will pay back what he has given." - Proverbs 19:17, NKJV*

Her name means "Heaven." Ironically, she has only experienced the contrary in the 8 years of her life. Jannat is a cute little girl with shabby clothes and unkempt hair. She was first brought to my outpatient department by the community team, with severe skin infections and boils all over her body. I never expected that behind those innocent looks, there were untold horrors and pain.

Many of us would not be able to comprehend what she has been through. She grew up not knowing who her father was, lived with a mother who was forced into a job considered unacceptable by society, witnessed her mother being killed by a stranger, been through a dark night holding her mother's lifeless limp body in her arms begging for money to bury her and do the last rites by herself, and finally, left alone on the unfriendly streets of the town with no one in this world, to survive all by herself. Can life be any more horrifying than this?

The little Braveheart resolved to live alone, begging and living off the streets. She begged for that day and lived for that day with nothing planned for tomorrow. She learned ways to survive, sniffing glue containing toluene, a hazardous chemical which apparently thousands of street children use to suppress hunger, induce sleep over the pains and struggles of life, and to withstand the cold nights. She found this way easier and cheaper to deal with her hunger and sleep, rather than to struggle and starve. When she spoke, she sounded like an adult because life deprived her of her childhood. In the midst of all this pain, Jannat would help out another old, blind beggar daily in crossing the road and feeding him from the little she gets. A huge lesson for a world that only knows to seek than to serve.

One soul responded to her, and instead of just dropping a coin and getting on with life, took time to talk to her. This was the first step for the team to resolve to help her. She was rescued, taken care of, and finally, a safe home was arranged. Hopefully, her life would not be the same anymore, and she would forget the past as a nightmare and have a better tomorrow.

Millions of Jannats are out there in our country. Many times, we become complacent with just feeling sorry and not doing anything more. Can we take it a step further? Can each one adopt or foster or at least support one little one? Our response might be just a drop in the ocean, but surely will be a blessing for that one person. Instead of just being engrossed in our own lives, running day and night, can we pause for a moment because there might be a Jannat out there on the verge of breaking, and you might be the very person God intended to use.

# HE IS NEAR...

## Ann Mary Thomas, MD

As he walked out of the hospital with his frail nine-year-old son, he shook his head in disbelief. What a roller coaster month it was! Who would've thought that boarding the flight to India for a vacation would change their lives forever? One evening, their son looked extremely tired and was unable to make conversation. The next thing, he was critically hospitalized, had an organ replacement surgery, and was battling life and death for the next 20-odd days. Tears, prayers, sleepless days, nights, and thirty days later, he was discharged, with two more tubes to be removed and an extensive list of medications to be given at home.

One month ago, he was competing with children older than him at debates and elocutions. A few months later, he was doing speech therapy and muscle-strengthening exercises. Everything had changed, and they'd just survived this storm as a family. A billion unanswered questions raged in his mind. The fact remains that sometimes one could never be prepared for what life can offer. Storms don't announce their arrival in advance. We get to know once they've arrived.

Boarding the flight to do a residency program in the 'City of Dreams,' I was simultaneously excited and nervous about my new house, a unique atmosphere, and a big step out of the comfort zone. It will only be a couple of years, I told myself. And completing the drill once already, I thought the second time would be easier.

Retrospectively, nothing prepared me for what was to unfold over the next few months. Experiencing the ruthless healthcare corporate environment was different.

I was in the middle of a storm, unable to find a footing or focus on my calling. I was left emotionally overwhelmed, gasping, reaching for familiar souls to help, give advice, or pray to help me survive.

What do you do when everything you do is challenged? Not one day, but almost every day? What do you do when your purpose is called into question? Somewhere amid this chaos, I couldn't hear my voice anymore, couldn't understand why anymore, and couldn't hear my soul anymore. I was exhausted. One day, nearing my end of hope, my disappointment and rage asked, "Do I even know who I am?" My husband gently looked into my eyes to echo what God was trying to convey from the beginning: Remember who you are! You are a child of God! I looked at him, assimilating what mattered. The only identity I needed was my identity as a redeemed child of God. Then the storm inside me abruptly halted. I took a break, retreating to the scriptures to hear from my Maker, I sat still as His love flooded my soul and tears streamed down my face. God who seemed far away for several months was close.

There was beauty in that moment I couldn't put into words. I was assured God never makes a mistake with His placement or my daily challenges. He knows precisely what He hopes to achieve through my season of life. Putting my fears and doubts and myriad of questions at His feet, I was reminded of this verse: *"...and he marked out their appointed times in history and the boundaries of their lands. God did this so that they would seek him and perhaps reach out for him and find him, though he is not far from any one of us. For in him we live and move and have our being." (Acts 17:26-27, NIV)*

On a short visit to CMC (Christian Medical College) Hospital in Ludhiana, an excerpt caught my eye echoing the founder's refrain, *'My work is for a King'*. I was reminded as I walked into my circumstances of my identity as a child of the Most High King, whom I sought to please alone. My focus had changed. As dark clouds passed and the sun rose, as it rained and poured, I marveled in disbelief at the story God was weaving through me. For most of my life, I've believed His presence moves ahead of me, but then I realized, as David sang his psalm, His goodness and mercy will also follow me...all of the days of my life. As I write this, I recall a familiar tune:

> *"Be still and know*
> *That the Lord is in control*
> *Be still my soul*
> *Stand and watch as giants fall...*
> *I won't be afraid*
> *You don't let go*
> *Be still my heart and know*
> *I won't be afraid"*

Dear reader, are your circumstances a rude shock? Or are you in a storm, wondering where your God is? Are you burnt out? Take heart, for He is there in the furnace, walking with you. Hold on to His hand, and remember you are His. His goodness and mercy will follow you. The world can challenge everything about you; all that matters is your assurance in Christ. And yes, He is in control. As the verse reminds us, *'In Him we live and move and have our being.'* Friend, He is not far from any of us *—Elohei Makarov.*

# HOME

## Ann Thomas, MD

All of us are born with this yearning for 'home.' Sometimes, we spend a lifetime trying to figure it out.

Recently, as I walked into the isolation room of the pediatric ICU, I met the smiling face of 4-year-old Akhil. Akhil had been diagnosed a few weeks back with a bad form of blood cancer. Nothing more to be done. He was being given palliative care, meaning support him till he succumbs. He certainly didn't look like it as I walked in to collect his medical history. He first gave me the 'Can you be trusted?' look, and then once he'd decided I could be taken into his confidence, he smiled with a twinkle in his eye. Suddenly, the chaos of the PICU outside the isolation room didn't matter anymore. I sat down beside him and asked him a basic question. "Hey, how are you?" The smile didn't cease as he replied,' "I'm good. I have cancer. But I'm going home."

That statement was a little too disconcerting for my sleep-deprived mind to process...my mind went " "Wait... did he just tell me his prognosis as well? Or did he just say he wants a DAMA order(discharge against medical advice)?"

So I asked him, like I'm a 4-year-old and he's the boss, "Home is where da?" He places his small hand in mine, looks at me like I have a long way to reach his understanding, and says, "See Chechi (elder sister), it's okay if you can't treat me because I'll be home in heaven with Jesus. That's where I actually came from. Will you pray with me today?"

As I held his hand and prayed with little Akhil in the PICU that night, I realized the truth in what Jesus said, "Unless you become like little children, you will not enter the Kingdom of God."

Wisdom doesn't always belong with the grey-haired. Born in one country, brought up in another, and then finding my vocation in a state with a different culture, if you ask me, where's home? I'll take some time to answer that one. But homesickness strikes often, and so does the yearning to belong somewhere. So, on one of those homesick days, I decided to go "home," where my parents lived. Guess what – 'homesickness' didn't go away. I spent time with my closest friends but had no luck there either. Finally, after I'd exhausted my available options, I knelt to spend some time with the Maker. Needless to say, it wasn't a long time before I felt at home.

That day, I realized what Akhil told me- home is not in the mountains or by the seaside; it's not where family is or where your entire lifetime was spent; it's not in the arms of your lover or with your closest friends- it's where your God is. In His presence, there you're best at home. Home's heaven. And that's what our hearts ache for. And this lifetime is the journey towards. And that was little Akhil's hope and joy.

*"My home is heaven. I'm just traveling through this world." Billy Graham.*

# THE CHOICE

## Ann Mary Thomas, MD

*"...yet I will rejoice in the LORD; I will
be joyful in God my Savior."
(Habakkuk 3:18, NIV)*

**P**re-rounds. The early morning rush was on to finish
everything before the consultants came. I took my exam
sheet and walked into room number 5 to a very peaceful-
looking mother. As we got talking about her one-year-old's
diagnosis, my heart sank lower and lower, with my mind a
tangled mess of questions and emotions- the unfairness
of it all, the injustice to this family, the pain. What could
you possibly say to this family?

Her baby had advanced stage malignancy with a
superimposed infection. For five minutes, my mind couldn't
get past this information. As I walked out after completing
my examination, I couldn't help but go over the mother's
words when I asked her how she was coping. She replied,
"I'll make the most of my time with her. Tell me what's the
plan for today, doctor." There was no blaming anyone, no
self-pity, no wondering what the future held for her; she

had chosen to take one day at a time. She chose her attitude towards a circumstance she could do nothing about. Habakkuk chose his attitude.

There are days when I feel dizzy with endless possibilities of what could have been to what they are now. Don't get me wrong, right now is excellent, but my brain goes into overthinking modes, where looking through those glasses right now could be better. Do you understand what I mean? Many times, looking at our circumstances, it's easy to fall into a pattern of self-pity, entitlement, or rebellion.

I've caught myself with these patterns of thoughts on days when I feel overpowered and just want to sit around and sulk. Those days, we feel wronged by the world - our families, friends, upbringing, and everything associated with us. I have often wondered if I missed the train leading me to where God wanted me to be.

Circumstances might be trying or less than ideal-Maybe you feel manipulated into a situation and feel you deserve better, maybe this wasn't how you imagined your life would turn out, or you think you need more time, and yet you don't have it, perhaps you can't get over your great past, and what you have now is not anywhere close- I don't know...can you think of any more?

Sometimes, the injustice around you makes your blood boil. Occasionally, you wonder whether God sees it. A quote reads, "Accustom yourself to unreasonableness and injustice. Abide in peace in the presence of God, who sees all these evils more clearly than you do and who permits them. Be content with doing with calmness the little which depends upon yourself, and let all else be to you as if it were no."

Reread it. And read it slowly.

Around the time we married, someone jokingly advised me, ' There may be days in your life when you wonder whether you're with the right person. I strongly advise you on those days to glance at the other name on your marriage certificate. That's exactly whom God meant you to be with - for better or worse.' Similarly, most days, we just have to rest and trust that God has us exactly where He would want us to be. He is all-powerful, after all.

My prayer over the last few months has been that God would help me clean out my messy thought life and give me a heart of discernment. God has been teaching me the power of choosing my attitude toward whatever circumstance. Choosing joy over misery, trusting God even when it doesn't make sense, obeying even if it's hard, and being kind to other colleagues even when it feels like they don't get you. Choosing an attitude of faith.

As I spent time in God's presence, I lay to rest the need to know when the storm would end. It sufficed to know more intimately, my God who controlled the storm.

*"My life is but a weaving.*
*Between my God and me;*
*I see the seams, the tangles,*
*But He sees perfectly.*
*He knows, He loves, He cares,*
*Nothing this truth can dim;*
*He gives His very best to those*
*Who chose to walk with Him." (Grant C. Tullar)*

May God enable you, dear reader, as we navigate another year, to choose your attitude towards your circumstances, knowing that the Lord we trust in has it all in His hands. He's weaving the story - yours and mine - and He's not done yet.

# HE MUST BECOME GREATER

## Bettina Thomas, DO

The integral moment that pushed me toward pediatrics occurred during my first year of medical school. As I packed my barely touched stethoscope with a fresh pair of scrubs, I started feeling anxious about my upcoming trip to Guatemala. Although I was eagerly looking forward to an exciting new experience, I wondered what a first-year medical student could bring to the table. I arrived in Zacapa, Guatemala, at Hope of Life International. Although I had been on mission trips before—once to an orphanage in Tijuana and a three-month venture in Africa to remote villages—this was my first medical mission. In the weeks leading up to the trip, I nervously brushed up on my newly acquired physical exam skills and googled common medical phrases in Spanish. During my week in Guatemala, we traveled to three local villages. We set up makeshift clinics in old school buildings and abandoned facilities.

As we drove into our first location in a caravan of school buses, I noticed a long stretch of people expectantly waiting in line. There were families, pregnant mothers, the elderly, and parents with babies at their hips. They all stood with small yellow slips in their hands, full of eagerness despite the scorching sun. As we drove up, our professor told us, "These people lined up are waiting to see you." I was overwhelmed: desperately wanting to help but ill-equipped to respond. This feeling quickly passed as I organized myself to the need. I had the opportunity to work in triage, where we took in patients and prioritized them on severity. My first patients were a family of five—a mother and her four kids. I asked questions and listened intently to each person, wielding my high school Spanish with the help of a translator. I performed ultrasounds on pregnant women, diagnosed a young girl with a seizure disorder, and met a woman with advanced breast cancer tearing through her skin. With a limited tool bag of basic medications, we sent each patient home after a quick evaluation to keep up with the number of people waiting. I was overwhelmed as each patient left my table, wishing I could do more. I wished I could follow up. I wished I could tell them I cared. I left that trip feeling more discouraged than recharged. I thought, "What was the purpose of dragging 50 young medical students, organizing for months and getting on a flight, when we were limited on the care we could provide onsite?"

It would be eight years before I would entertain another medical mission trip. This time, recently graduated from my pediatric residency, I had some years of clinical experience. We joined Lukes International's trip to Cambodia, and I thought surely this time I would have more to give. We boarded a long flight to Cambodia and, similar to Guatemala, set up tables waiting for our patients to be triaged. My first patients were two young sisters who just wanted to be examined. As the days went on, I encountered a young boy with an unusual rash and a newborn who never saw a doctor. On the second to last day of the trip I met another young boy with suspected tuberculosis and his father, who had tuberculosis for months, desperately coming to us for treatment. We rummaged through our pharmacy for any helpful medication yet finding none. Dejected, we walked back to this desperate father and son and said, "We don't have the medications you need." We pleaded with the father to let us help get him to a local hospital. The father adamantly refused, saying, "I would never be able to afford a hospital visit." We continued to beg and plead until eventually he walked away with his son back to their home. I stood there disheartened and helpless, watching them walk away. The week went by fast, and soon, I found myself back on the plane heading back to NY with an eerily similar feeling to when I left Guatemala. And again, I thought to myself, "What was the point? Did I even make a difference?"

It is a feeling I have grappled with for months. I went through medical school and subsequent training, hoping I could change people's lives. But the realization of the deeper purpose God had for me finally hit me. Whether I was a young, inexperienced medical student or a licensed pediatric attending, it didn't make a difference. The changes being made in the lives of these people I encountered in Guatemala and Cambodia had nothing to do with me. It was God moving *through* me, and it was God working *in* them. It was the name of God being glorified. My skills and abilities were merely tools God used to accomplish his purposes. I incorrectly counted success by my abilities to heal people's medical ailments. But the healing was being done on a deeper level than my mind could grasp. Now, as a practicing physician, when feelings of doubt creep in, I am reminded of my experience through these trips that God should be greater, and I should be less. As providers and medical professionals, we have spent much of our careers and educational journeys trying to reach the next step. But our purpose in these roles is not measured by our medical accomplishments but rather by our openness to let God use us to build his kingdom and to bring healing to his world.

# WHO'S DRIVING?

## Jones P. Thomas, MD

I enjoy knowing how things work. Though my wife laughs at me, I enjoy reading through instruction manuals for our refrigerator or any new technological gadget we purchase. Give me a map and instructions, and I will figure out the rest. My wife humors me when I comb through these instruction manuals, exploring how to make things better and more efficient with the technology available. With this mindset, a logical career choice would be engineering. However, career aside, a more critical manual was missing my life's instruction manual. Fast forward to my wedding, and I was still uncertain about reading my life's roadmap.

The verse we chose for our wedding was Jeremiah 29:11,*NIV* - "For I know the plans I have for you, says the Lord, plans to prosper you and not to harm you, plans to give you a hope and a future." For most people, this verse is comforting. But for me, this powerful promise felt inefficient. Why wouldn't God tell me His plan so I could make it work? To me, it sounded like God had the map and yet insisted on making me drive blindfolded! This story is my testimony, a journey showing me I am never in the driver's seat; God is driving the whole time!

Born and raised in a Malayalee Pentecostal household, I grew up surrounded by all things God. Our church in north India started in our home, and our deep familial involvement with the church continued throughout the years in various forms. After moving to the United States, I was involved in our small local church from a young age. I started operating slide presentations with lyrics on an overhead projector, moving on to setting up and breaking down sound equipment, and eventually leading in various roles, including music ministry and Sunday school. Through all this, I felt I was in tune with God and His purpose for my life.

As I was finishing high school, suddenly I was unsure of my purpose, or was it God's purpose for my life or career? In the most cliché way, I bounced back and forth between medicine and engineering, eventually deciding on engineering and securing admission to a local engineering college. As I was in the middle of my senior year of high school, I had a unique opportunity to return to India. My uncle, the late Pastor M.K. Babu, whose evangelism and ministry were well established in north India, was planning to travel with outreach ministries to several northern states of India for several months, even to the neighboring country of Nepal. I learned of this opportunity, and with just a few weeks' notice and a "now-or-never" attitude, I decided to defer my admission to college for a year and go to India.

My time in India was nothing short of life-changing. I left the United States with a fairly open plan, and the trip lasted nine months. During this time, we traveled to eight north Indian states, including as far east as Arunachal Pradesh and Nepal. Among other events, we hosted medical mission teams from the United States, providing local logistics in several remote regions. Watching these health professionals delivering care to folks in extremely poverty-stricken and undereducated settings flipped a switch in my mind about my priorities. Previously I was convinced through my work as an engineer I would give back to the community and find fulfillment. However, after seeing immense medical need, and disposition required to deliver care, a slight tug pulled in my heart, perhaps this was my true calling and channel for fulfillment.

I came back to the United States facing a problem. I had an admission spot in an engineering program with a reasonably mapped-out career path. But instead, pursuing medicine would be to throw caution to the wind and lean heavily into God's leading. Medicine would be a multi-decade commitment, with many hurdles, each of which could completely derail the eventual goal. Many students started college in a "premed" track, but only a few became physicians. To be eligible for medical school, I would have to finish a bachelor's degree with a good GPA and a strong MCAT score. Then I'd have to be accepted into a medical school, graduate medical school, pass the USMLE, match into a residency, complete the residency training, to be then capped off by board exams in whatever specialty I chose, if I even found a specialty I liked! In retrospect, perhaps the Holy Spirit hid some of the significance of these challenges, or I probably would never have headed down this path! Thank God for his mercy.

Fast forward 15 years, and I can reflect on my life and say God was always on and by my side. I found my passion in medicine in vascular surgery, serving a population with significant needs. Now, when I evaluate gangrenous feet or the effects of severe peripheral vascular disease from smoking or poorly controlled cardiovascular risk factors, I think back to the impoverished and uneducated people in the medical mission camps in India. It seemed improbable what a full circle my life would make: much is different in the Midwestern United States from rural India, but in reality, much is the same. I'm grateful to have been a passenger on this journey and look forward to future adventures.

# HE IS IN CONTROL

## Mathew Thomas, MD

The scene is still vivid in my mind as if it were yesterday. It was past midnight, and I was in the middle of a challenging double lung transplantation on a very sick patient about 70 years old. This operation was by no means straightforward, made more difficult by the patient's advanced age. Many institutions performing lung transplants have an upper age limit of 70 years because of the morbidity associated with it in older patients. We did not consider advanced age an absolute contraindication but were fully aware of its implications. An uncomplicated double lung transplant can be completed in about 6-10 hours but can take longer in sick patients and those with complex pathology. A few years into my practice as a new cardiothoracic surgeon attending, I had an extra burst of enthusiasm about doing these significant operations.

We had completed the first lung, the right side, and reperfused it by releasing the clamps controlling the right pulmonary artery and veins. The lung was then reinflated, a beautiful sight as always, the flaccid grayish balloon gradually puffing up and turning pink as blood gushed through the alveolar capillaries. Medical students and other first-time observers often exclaim with astonishment at this memorable moment, only rivaled by the first beat of a newly transplanted heart. For me, it reminded me of how fearfully and wonderfully we are created (Psalm 139:14) and how finely tuned things have to be for life to happen, a dance so perfectly orchestrated that it underscores the limitless mind of the Intelligent Designer.

Six hours is a number every lung transplant surgeon keeps in mind. This is called the cold ischemic time, beyond which, if not reperfused, the graft suffers damage that could be permanent. The countdown clock starts when the donor heart is stopped and includes the time to procure and transport the lungs, which may take 2-3 hours. We were halfway when we restored blood flow to the right lung, leaving us about another 3 hours to remove the sick left lung and attach the new one, which is usually sufficient time in an uncomplicated case.

After removing the left lung without any problems, I placed the new lung into the patient's left chest. Lung transplant involves creating three connections between the recipient and the donor's lung: the bronchus (breathing tube), artery, and vein. We finished the bronchial connection without a hitch. Things were going well, and we could finish with the other two connections in about 30 minutes. My assistant gently lifted and pulled the heart to the right so I could see the left pulmonary vein and artery tucked deep under the heart. I began sewing the veins first, which are the farthest to reach, when the anesthesiologist signaled things were about to go south. "He doesn't like it," he said, "His pressure is dropping." I wasn't too concerned since this is not unusual when the heart is lifted or compressed. The heart usually recovers in a minute or two after it is moved back into its place, and the procedure often resumes. We repositioned the heart, but there was another more serious problem this time. The first lung was showing signs of failure, called primary graft dysfunction (PGD). This manifests as fluid in the lungs (pulmonary edema), which may be mild or severe. We knew we were dealing with a severe case of PGD when, within a few minutes, copious watery fluid started pouring out of the breathing tube - the patient was drowning. It was only a matter of minutes before the lung would become stiff, and the right side of his heart would stop first, followed by the left, causing a full cardiac arrest. We needed to go on cardiopulmonary bypass ("go on pump") emergently to save his life, which typically can be accomplished in 5 to 7 minutes. The team was well-experienced in dealing with such emergencies and immediately began setting up to go on a pump when suddenly the patient arrested (i.e., cardiopulmonary function stopped), causing a quick change of plans. My assistant began massaging the heart, squeezing it with his hand, while I continued to prepare to insert large cannulas (tubes) to go on the pump. First, I had to place sutures in the aorta and the heart, not an easy task when the heart is being forcibly massaged, almost like writing on a lined notebook while riding in an off-road jeep.

The emotions and stress of the moment are hard to describe. It is pretty easy to panic in a situation like this and lose control. As the 'captain of the ship,' the team would immediately sense any loss of confidence on my part, which could lead to chaos in the operating room. Overpowering thoughts of failure came over me; death seemed like an inevitable outcome, and I would have to tell the family that their loved one did not make it. I would have to explain this death at the mortality and morbidity conference in front of a jury of my peers, but above all; I would have failed the patient who trusted me to get him through this. The thought was almost paralyzing – of all the patient deaths that I have encountered, perhaps the most surrealistic is the intraoperative death. Nearly all transplant patients go into surgery expecting to be given another chance at life, and so do their families and surgeons. In this case, even if the patient survived the operation, there was no guarantee that he would leave the hospital alive. I still needed to finish transplanting the left lung with time running out, and I could only hope that the right lung would recover.

As the moribund thoughts overwhelmed me, I knew there was only one thing left to do - I had to turn to the never-ending source of wisdom and life, the Lord God. There have been many such instances in my life, both in and out of the operating room, where I felt I was at the end of my human abilities or wisdom. In such situations, remembering my calling and identity as a child of the Creator, God has been an anchor in the storm.

"Even though I walk through the valley of the shadow of death, I will fear no evil, for you are with me" (Psalm 23:4a ESV). "The name of the LORD is a strong tower; the righteous man runs into it and is safe" (Prov 18:10 ESV). "For when I am weak, then I am strong" (2 Cor 12:10b NKJV). These words ran through my mind, overcoming the darkness that seemed to win at first.

I called out silently, "Lord, I need You to take over here. Holy Spirit, thank You for being here with me". One verse in particular that the Holy Spirit reminds me of when I am facing an insurmountable challenge regardless of the situation is 1 Cor 2:16b NKJV: "But we have the mind of Christ." As children of God saved by grace, we have been given access to the very heart of the Father, including His wisdom and understanding. I was also reminded by the Holy Spirit that "I can do all things through Christ who strengthens me" (Phil 4:13 NKJV). As I slightly prayed this silently, I felt the peace of God come over me in a very palpable way, and it became clear that He was in control. He was always in control – I just needed a reminder. We were able to complete the operation successfully, and the patient survived.

As I left the operating room praising God for His deliverance, the chief anesthesiologist that night, who was also a believer, walked up to me. "Matt," he said, "when things were going down rapidly, I saw the look on your face and knew this was not going to end well." He told me that as the situation took a turn for the worse, he immediately called his wife, waking her up around 2 am, and asked her to pray for us. This was a stunning revelation for me! There is no doubt in my mind that this dear brother and his wife's prayer was instrumental in the deliverance we encountered that night, for the power of intercessory prayer should never be underestimated.

I have been reminded time and time again through adversities that God's promises never fail. His strength and wisdom are available for us in any challenge, and we must learn to apply them by faith. The realization that "we have the mind of Christ" has been one of the most empowering facts in my Christian walk and has had limitless implications for daily living. Imagine how different life would be if our hearts beat in synchrony with the heart of God and our minds knew His thoughts: if we could fully feel His pain for a sick and dying world; if we could hear his heartache for the downtrodden and those in despair; if we could draw on the hope that He brings when all hope is gone.

When I saw the patient a few months later in the outpatient clinic, I praised God for His faithfulness, especially for the faithful believers' family.

# IN THE WAITING

## Elsa Vadakekut, DO

The moment a baby was delivered had always been sacred to me. When that first shaky intake of air fills a tiny chest, and then a pause that was sometimes quick, other times a little longer. As if the infant was asking, "Now what?" Waiting in anticipation for that screaming exhalation because it was the first proof of life, the start of a journey, and evidence of God's creative power placed right in my hands.

The delivery of a stillborn was also sacred. But those anguished moments were more of a quiet reverence, a tragic reminder of the sanctity of life. Amid the spinning chaos of the OR that day, there was a sudden hush. The slick, lifeless infant demanded a consecrated silence of us. It was a boy I saw. Being a week shy of the third trimester, his skin was still a translucent purple, his eyelids fused, but otherwise, he looked normal. His death had been recent; his body had no signs of deterioration yet.

When the patient had first come into L&D complaining of a headache, the nurse quickly came to find me, the OB/GYN on drop-in call that day, after she had not been able to find fetal heart tones. A young African-American female, Jehovah's Witness, in the 27th week of her first pregnancy. "I'm taking serial BP's, but they all have been high, 160's/100's," she told me. I jumped up from where I had been sitting in the doctor's dictation area, my chest tight with foreboding. This nurse was experienced; a fetal demise was likely if she could not find a heartbeat. As I slid the ultrasound probe over the tight brown skin of the patient's slightly protruding belly, my fear was confirmed.

I gently explained to the young woman that her baby had died, emphasizing that she could have done nothing to prevent it; patients often blamed themselves. The woman blankly looked at me and said nothing. I presumed she was in shock, a common reaction. But when I asked if she understood, she calmly turned to me and said, "I don't believe you. You're lying." Although not a reaction I had seen before, I thought she was overwhelmed. I again pointed to the lack of movement in the fetal heart on the ultrasound, trying to explain. However, it was not until I had another ultrasound performed by a radiologist that she finally believed my diagnosis. I hoped with this corroboration that she would begin to trust me. But the opposite happened as the situation started to spiral downwards; she seemed to trust me less.

Initially, I had planned to induce labor, deliver the stillborn, and manage her preeclampsia. The young woman, however, had no intention of letting me do anything. She wanted to go home, and no matter what I or her nurse said, she refused to stay. She began bleeding from her vagina, a placental abruption; still, she demanded I let her go. Soon, I noticed bleeding from her gums; she was progressing to DIC, which would cause spontaneous bleeding throughout her body. I told her we had to do a C-section to prevent her from hemorrhaging to death, as her cervix was still closed, but she refused everything, including a transfusion. Instead, she asked, "Are you even a real doctor? Show me your license."

"Of course, I'm a real doctor! And I'm trying to help you. I know you may not understand everything right now, but please trust that I am doing my best to make you better," I had said, rather befuddled. She glowered at me and hissed, "I don't trust any of you." Then she yelled, "You killed my baby! And now you're trying to kill me!" The nurse and I looked at each other in disbelief. What was wrong with this woman? Why had she bothered coming to the hospital if she didn't think we would help her? To convince the patient, who was becoming progressively more unstable, to stay, I had the OB/GYN department chair and two anesthesiologists speak to her. She only looked at us with absolute loathing. It was not until she briefly passed out while signing papers to leave against medical advice that she finally agreed to our management plan; she also agreed to a transfusion. As our team ran the patient into the main OR, I prayed that God would do the miraculous for this woman and that she would see God at work through us.

After quickly clamping and cutting the thin cord, I gently passed the infant to the scrub tech, and the tempest of the OR returned. Immediately, I reached inside the woman's uterus and pulled out the placenta, barely attached due to the abruption. Blood poured from the uterine cavity as the anesthesiologist called out, "Pitocin is already going!" She was also squeezing the unit bag of blood, trying to replace it as fast as it was bleeding out. I quickly sutured the uterus closed and massaged the uterus between my hands, trying to remind it what to do. "See here, uterus," I thought, "You are supposed to clamp down! Work with me!" Typically, after the placenta is delivered, the uterus contracts, constricting large blood vessels and slowing blood loss. Instead, as soon as I stopped massaging, I could see her uterus become soft and balloon out, filling with blood. When I would squeeze down again, blood flowed between my fingers. She had uterine atony, not unexpected in a patient with preeclampsia, but I had been praying for a miracle. "Please, God," I silently begged as I barked out the obstetric hemorrhage protocol, "Make it stop bleeding; show her your goodness." We worked down the algorithm for postpartum hemorrhage, and I held my breath with each medication, praying in fevered silence as sweat trickled down my back under my surgical gown. As more units of blood and platelets were rushed in, I added another request to my relentless prayers, "Please, God, don't let her die."

The assisting physicians and I tried everything, from medications to surgical techniques, but the patient's bleeding refused to abate. Her abdomen continued to fill with blood as quickly as it was suctioned away. Eventually, we were at the end of the algorithm; there was nothing left but a hysterectomy to attempt to stop the blood loss. I was despairing because I did not want to do this to her, to remove her ability to have any other babies added to the memory of the one lifeless child she had born. She would never forgive me. With every intervention, I prayed to God to make it work, even praying in tongues under my breath, which my partners didn't notice as they loudly cursed the patient's noncooperative body. How dare she continue to bleed! So again, requesting wisdom from God Almighty, I asked my partners, "Any other ideas?" But weighing her death against a hysterectomy, I was only met with the same conclusion: the hysterectomy would have to be done. Now.

I called out the order to convert to a hysterectomy, and the nurses scrambled to get the necessary equipment already in the room, prepared for this potential eventuality. The anesthesiologist nodded, a whirling dervish behind the drape as she continued to work the massive transfusion protocol, infusing blood and giving orders to send more PRBCs, platelets, and fresh frozen plasma to keep my patient alive as I struggled over her gaping abdominal cavity. Any attempts to keep the use of blood products to a minimum in deference to her Jehovah's Witness beliefs had been left behind a long time ago; we were all just doing our best to keep this woman from going over the brink into the abyss. And through my mind, as I set to the task ahead with my heart thrashing in my chest, floated the thought, "God, where are you?"

Afterward, the same thought stayed with me through the night as I obsessively monitored her vitals. I had failed. My prayers to God to help me bring this woman through surgery without further complications and prove God's power had gone unanswered. She was alive, yes, but not only had she lost her baby, but she also would never have another biologically. On top of that, I had transfused ten units of blood, betraying her beliefs. I had done everything I could to save her, but would she want to live that life anymore? This was not how I had foreseen God would come through for me. I struggled to understand why my prayer had gone unanswered. Hadn't I had enough faith? Was I not a good enough surgeon to avoid this catastrophic outcome?

The following day, when I came into the ICU to do her postoperative rounds, I was sure that I would be met with the continuation of yesterday's calamity. Instead, she looked like a routine postoperative patient, not one that had recently faced death. I was amazed that while she still had HELLP and high blood pressure, her lab values, and vital signs were already trending in the right direction. However, any hope for a different attitude towards me was swiftly dashed the moment her eyes met mine. She glared at me in silence, refusing to utter one word. I explained everything that had happened during her surgery and asked if she had any questions. Her mouth formed a tight line in reply.

I tried to express sympathy for the overwhelming loss she was facing and understanding of the grief she had to process. She closed her eyes and clenched her jaw. Accepting that she needed space, I left and returned to my office. On the way there, I ran into Dr. Lee, the anesthesiologist who had helped me with her surgery. She threw her arms around me and said, "I can't believe how well she is doing today! I can't believe it! I was sure she would have acute lung injury or circulatory overload after all that blood, but she is perfect! The whole department was shocked! I told her that God MUST have some big plans for her!" Dr. Lee told me that most hospital staff had learned of this patient's case, and everyone was in awe that she had survived. I just shook my head at her and said dumbly, "But she won't even look at me! She just blames me for the hysterectomy and everything." Dr. Lee cocked her head and replied, "No, there's something else going on with her...the way she acted yesterday and all, I think she's angrier with herself. I told her this morning she is lucky to even be alive, but you know, sometimes patients just don't know enough to understand why we have to do some things." I shrugged, "Yeah, yeah, I know," dryly adding, "It doesn't feed my God-complex though."

She laughed and, turning away, began speed walking down the hall, raising her hand to wave goodbye. Without turning around, she called out, "Ahh, you did your best! But it's still in God's hands, girl!" As I spoke to other nurses and physicians, her words rattled through my mind. No one could believe this woman's progress over a few days. Meanwhile, I kept trying to get my stubborn patient to speak one word to me. She was truculent with all the ICU nurses, so I wasn't the only one, but at least she would mumble terse replies to them. For me, all she had was a cold glare. I understood that waking up to discover you no longer had a uterus at the age of 25 was a complicated thing to wrap your head around; complex psychological issues were involved, with anger and grief being very typical. But usually, there was some recognition of the surgeon's efforts.

I struggled more than usual because I felt I deserved her resentment. I knew she was already angry with me for diagnosing her with a stillborn; forcing massive transfusions and sterility upon her in my efforts to save her just added to my "wrongdoing." She wasn't healed the way I had hoped. But as I continued to care for this woman, God began to teach me a different lesson. I began to see that her mistrust of me reflected my lack of trust in God. I was asking God for help, but I really believed it was up to me. I wanted God to use me, but I wanted it done my way. I gave God lip service, saying my patients were in his hands, but I remained anxious because I didn't have the faith to wait for his plan to unfold. But now, I started asking myself, how would it look to trust God with this patient? I began to see that it is in the waiting that faith grows enough to birth a miracle. True faith was learned in waiting, surrendering my need to God's sovereignty, even though things didn't happen as I planned.

The day she was to be sent home; I wasn't sure of what else to say after going over her discharge instructions. But standing at her bedside, I said, "You know, I didn't want to do a hysterectomy, but if I had to do it again, it would be the same. I know it's a big loss, but you are worth more than just your ability to have children."

She was still silent, but she seemed less angry than before. Suddenly, tears began to run down her face, dripping from her chin onto her hospital gown. "I should have died," she said, shaking her head. "Having a baby, unmarried...My momma said I..." faltering, she continued, her voice strangled, "I deserve to be punished." I gently squeezed my hand on hers until she met my gaze. "The fact that you are still alive and breathing without any other issues is not only a miracle, it's evidence that God has you here for a purpose. I don't know why you are going through all this, but I do know that by going through it, you will be stronger. And in time, even transformed into someone better."

This is a lesson I continue to learn, professionally and personally. It is difficult to surrender control and allow myself to be led beside those still waters. Too often, I keep such a tight grip on my plan that I burn out instead of finding rest in God's sovereignty. I forget that God's primary objective is an eternal one. The outcome he desires for my patient may be one I fail to understand. Struggle, failure, and suffering are all part of the human condition, but only by undergoing God's refinement and enduring through them are we transformed from the natural to the supernatural. Through waiting for God to work, we begin to really know God and trust him enough to enter his rest. It's only going through that journey that we are truly healed.

# HEAVEN ON EARTH

## Bessie Thomas-Varughese, OD

They say the "eyes are the windows to the soul," As metaphorical as it sounds, I think I've come to appreciate that saying in my years as a clinical optometrist. God has given me a unique position to spend a considerable amount of time talking about life outside my patients' eyes. It often starts with "How are you feeling today," to quickly blend into a conversation about faith or suffering. And while I've had many divine encounters in my office, even some miraculous moments, I will never forget the day Ms. S walked into my life. Ms. S was a new patient to me, and though she was clear she did not want to see me, God had different plans that day.

It was mid spring, and I in a challenging season of my own, when Ms. S came for her annual exam. She was born with cerebral palsy, and required two metal crutches against her forearms to walk and aid her mobility. She also came with a friend who assisted her to sit and stand. I went through her records before her visit and noticed that previous doctors did testing on her right eye, the good eye. The left eye had an obvious defect and seemingly didn't function well because of it. Within the first few minutes of examining, I realized she had reasonably good vision in the "bad" eye. While her eyes were dilating I ordered extra testing, difficult and inconvenient but warranted, since she never truly received a comprehensive exam on both eyes. I felt her previous providers assumed a low function of her left eye and inadequately assessed it.

After finishing the tests, Ms.S and her friend waited outside my office, and I could hear the frustration and disapproval in my patient's voice. "Why did I come to see this doctor? "They try'n to test this eye, but there's no good doing that. Doesn't she know this eye isn't so good anyway? Who does she think she is?"

She was loud and abrasive, and I thought, here goes another appointment I'll just have to get through as quickly as possible. I brought her back into my room; she was unaware of what I heard and I pretended to be unaware of what she said. She looked at me with haste as if I was wasting her time. I quickly finished my exam before sitting back to tell her my assessment.

"Ms. S, your eyes are in good condition... both." She looked at me, almost unbelieving, as if I had lied to her. I began to tell her that despite how it seemed to her, both her eyes functioned well, and although her left eye appeared defective, it's just as healthy as the right. As I explained further, she smiled and started whispering to her friend, "I gotta tell him, I gotta tell him. God is good!" Not knowing who she was referring to, I repeated after her, saying, "Yes, God is good." Then, I began to tell her about Romans 8:28 and how it resonated with me that week. She wanted to write the verse down, stating she couldn't wait to tell her brother, who is a pastor, and how happy he would be to hear the report about her eyes. I then asked her about her church, and she replied she hadn't gone since the pandemic, so I invited her and her friend to mine.

After giving her the address, I asked the Spirit to help me pray for her before she left my room. As soon as I held her hands to help her up from the chair, she rose extremely grateful, and to my surprise began to pray for *me* in the Spirit. She prayed loudly and I had to close my door, fearing my coworkers and staff would surely hear.

Spirit-led praise and prayer filled that room. After she prayed, she said words of encouragement I knew were from God. She spoke into my difficult season and encouraged me through it, and spoke the thoughts He had for me. It was an incredible moment standing hand in hand with tears streaming down our faces in awe of the Father's love for us. At the outset she didn't want to come to my office since I wasn't her regular doctor, but God told her to come and now she realized why.

I felt like an angel was sent to minister to me in an unlikely way, in an unlikely place. Her words strengthened me for that season, and I needed no more assurance that God was working things out for my good. It turned out no one else heard what happened in that room; I was the only witness to this moment of heaven on earth.

I keep in touch with Ms. S and her friend, Ms. Linda, as they continue to pray for me and encourage me with His love. Meeting them has become a remarkable moment in my life and a constant reminder of God's goodness and love towards us.

I reflect on this particular moment as a witness of Christ sent into His mission field. He astonishes me by His concern that He would be merciful to send people my way to show His heart for me. *"The LORD be exalted, who delights in the prosperity of His servant."* Psalm 35:27, *NASB*